MiG Master

MiG Master
The Story of the F-8 Crusader

Barrett Tillman

SECOND EDITION

NAVAL INSTITUTE PRESS
Annapolis, Maryland

First edition published by the Nautical and Aviation
Publishing Company of America, 1980

The paper used in this publication meets the
minimum requirements of American National
Standard for Information Sciences—Permanence of
Paper for Printed Library Materials,
ANSI Z39.48-1984.

Library of Congress Cataloging-in-Publication Data

Tillman, Barrett.
    MiG master: the story of the F-8 Crusaders /
  Barrett Tillman.—
  2nd ed.
       p.   cm.
  Includes bibliographical references.
  ISBN 0-87021-585-X :
  1. Crusader (Jet fighter plane)   I. Title.
UG1242.F5T55   1990
358.4'3—dc20   89-13628
                                         CIP

Printed in the United States of America

9 8 7 6 5 4 3 2 1

For Beverly Barrett Tillman
Who tolerates two aviators in the family

Contents

Foreword

This book is a factual, nuts-and-bolts record of the life of an airplane. It is also a critique of our national policy vis-à-vis air warfare, with particular emphasis on lessons learned in Vietnam. But it is much more than either of these; it is a rare military history. All too infrequently do our military historians focus on a particular mission, on a particular group of men, over the relatively short time span of a quarter century. Except when one does, and does so not only with thoroughness but with the authentic re-creation of firsthand experiences in the style of a Barrett Tillman, the lessons behind the success and failures, the victories and defeats of major military enterprises, usually go unnoticed and die in the dusty "unit history" archives of the Defense Department.

MiG Master is the history of a romantic first-of-a-kind generation of dogfighting carrier pilots who, while being told that their art and craft belonged to a bygone age, brought that craft up through its development years, took it into battle, and showed the experts that a fighting heart and a rambunctious steed still can carry the day in an age of high technology. That the steed was rambunctious was clear to the Crusader generation from their first briefing in the mid-1950s. As an LSO, I can attest that it is as demanding an airplane in the groove as any the navy has ever put aboard carriers. It may have been the first for which preselection of pilots on the basis of their reflexes and agility on the "handlebars" was advisable.

And in those early days, the Crusader was in need of refinements. Tillman recalls for us the years of frustration and experimentation spent in making the gun system serviceable and repeatable in the twenty- and thirty-thousand-foot gunnery patterns. Who among us who made the 1950s cruises can forget the hazards of the weak landing gear and the fixes upon fixes necessary to make the wheels stay on after a high sink-rate "plant" into the wires? I flew Crusaders through five WestPac cruises, and on the first two (USS *Midway*, 1958 and 1959) I made it squadron policy to bring them all the way down the glideslope and into the wires, holding a steady "one ball low" on the lens to take a couple of degrees off the deck impact angle.

Technologists will find a detailed description of these problems early in this volume, and the story of latter-day airframe and engine modifications for the foreign market at the end. But for old and new fighter pilots, for the casual reader of today, and perhaps even for the cults of tomorrow, the middle of the book is where it all happens. There, in authentic fighter pilot terms, Barrett Tillman takes us through the key actions of the early years of the Vietnam War (1964–1968), when the Crusader generation— by then lieutenant commanders and commanders with a couple of thousand hours in type, handled those rambunctious steeds with scarcely a glance in the cockpit. Directing their wingmen through the constantly changing three-dimensional puzzles of air combat maneuvering, they wove arabesques of maneuver in the vertical plane, that natural habitat of the gun fighter, taking more MiGs out of the sky than any other airplane in our nation's arsenal.

The book was immensely informative to me, because I spent three of those five years from 1964–1968 hearing the air actions from the ground in Hanoi, not knowing who the major players were "up there." Hardly a name is mentioned in this book that does not bring back memories—sometimes laughs, sometimes sadness for splashed "no-shows" at prison camp, but always memories of admiration and pride. I had served in many of the squadrons accounted for. VF-211 and VF-24 were setting their MiG shootdown records over the Hanoi power plant and elsewhere during a busy and trying summer of 1967—the summer of a tough purge and broken bones in the Hoa Lo Jail below. (I had deployed as ops officer of 211 and as exec of 24.) My old command, VF-51, shone frequently, and particularly in the summer of 1968. What a morale boost it would have been for me to know that, during my summer in a little dungeon known as Alcatraz! It was with particular pride that I read about the grand battle performances of Chuck Ludden (of VMF-212) and Dick Bellinger (VF-162). Both their squadrons were in my wing when I was shot down as CAG-16. It was VMF-212 that came up with the idea of carrying a 2,000-pound bomb under each wing—which we did regularly *without* BuAer authorization, taking the cat shot with half a fuel load to stay below the launch gross weight redline.

It is perhaps understandable that this foreword is hardly the detached, objective sort of piece that one expects to introduce a volume of history. My position is rather one of emotion—love and attachment to the men and the enterprise it describes. Moreover, the F-8 was not, as I saw it, a "cool," "analytical," or "detached" program. It staked out territory at the cutting edge of technology. We who volunteered into the program from the start (and most in it did so) never went on the assumption that "handbook" procedures were going to solve the problems that would surely follow in the wake of such a bold step forward in performance. To be an F-8 pilot was from the start to be emotionally involved in making it work with human initiative and improvisation.

That spirit carried on into combat, and became a killer instinct. For the armchair strategist who believes that modern weapon systems sink or swim solely on the basis of programmed responses to computer-induced stimuli, let him contemplate the kind of automation one would need to duplicate the experience-based intuitive deductions, the innate judgment of risk trade-offs, the calculated unpredictability, the endurance, and the conditioned reflexes of the professional Crusader jocks whose feats are described by Barrett Tillman. My hat is off to the MiG killers who, as the author correctly states, "enjoy a status that neither rank nor decorations can match."

James B. Stockdale
Vice Admiral, USN(Ret.)

Preface

In naval aviation, an important stopover on the road to progress was Vought's F8U Crusader. The F-8 retains an honored spot in carrier flying, as it propelled the navy "from the third row into the front seat" of military aviation. For no other navy aircraft had the Vought's potential at the time of its appearance. Primarily, that potential was speed: the great leap from transonic to supersonic flight. The F8U was the world's first production airplane to exceed 1,000 miles per hour in level flight, and the fact that this record fell to a carrier aircraft was all the more spectacular.

Originally intended as an air superiority fighter, the Crusader eventually filled a variety of missions: photo-reconnaissance, strike, and engineering testbed. In this respect it rivaled its famous ancestor, the F4U Corsair, in versatility. And longevity. Thirty years after its first flight, the F-8 still was employed as a photo aircraft by the U.S. Navy; as a carrier fighter by the French; and as a land-based fighter by the Philippine Air Force.

But the Crusader's primary function was fulfilled during the Vietnam War. For eight bitter years, navy and marine F-8 squadrons were engaged almost daily over North or South Vietnam. Much has been said of the "failure" of airpower in that ill-directed, mismanaged conflict, and of necessity a study of the Crusader will in part become a study of the war itself. There is bitterness and resentment in the pages dealing with Vietnam, but not without reason. For bitterness and resentment are part and parcel of the Vietnam War.

Documenting the F-8's Vietnam activities has not been easy. If anything, it has been downright difficult. In sharp contrast to the detailed, well-organized after-action reports of World War II, the navy did little to record its role in Vietnam. And those reports that were compiled—frequently after the war—remain classified because of the Crusader's postwar operational status. Therefore, this volume cannot deal with the subject to the extent originally desired. But *MiG Master* is the first in-depth examination of any aircraft engaged in Vietnam, and later writers will perhaps benefit from what progress has been made here.

A new language has grown up around jet aircraft in the last 40 years, and relatively few of the familiar terms or designations remain from the 1940s. Therefore, a glossary has been included for those who have not yet made the mental transition to jets. The Crusader, like most navy aircraft of the fifties and sixties, bore two designations, and the text follows that trend accordingly. The original designation of F8U is employed up to late 1962, when the Department of Defense standardized all military aircraft designations. After that, the contemporary F-8 appellation is used.

Airspeeds generally are given in nautical miles per hour, though statute miles (15 percent less than knots) are specified where appropriate. Mach numbers have not been widely used, but are unavoidable when dealing with supersonic aircraft.

One small measure of what the F-8 has meant to naval aviation may be found in the logbook of one contributor to this volume. Retired for many years, this aviator made his first carrier landing in a Great Lakes TG-1—a lumbering, open-cockpit biplane capable of 110 mph. That was in 1936. Barely 20 years later he recorded his final "trap" in a Mach-2 Crusader. Thus, the F-8 may serve as a gauge of the headlong rush of aviation technology—at a rate that has been breath-taking.

MiG Master

Vought's Star
Is Born

1

British aviation writer Bill Gunston remembers "a typical Russian cocktail party" in Paris about 1962. Gunston doesn't recall the occasion—possibly a celebration of a Soviet space triumph for the aviation press—but he does remember he was "amazed to find a few people present who had interesting things to say." One of them was a high-ranking Soviet officer dressed in civilian clothes.

During the conversation, Gunston asked which Western aircraft the Eastern bloc most respected. After a brief pause, the Russian made his choice: Chance Vought's Crusader. The F8U, he said, was likely to appear at almost any spot on the globe and establish air superiority.[1]

If praise from one's enemy is the highest praise of all, this opinion represents the supreme compliment. But the Russian apparently knew his subject. The Crusader, being a carrier-based aircraft, could indeed show up almost anywhere. And, being among the handful of naval fighters that have equaled or bettered the performance of their land-based adversaries, the F8U was fully capable of controlling the sky within its reach.

By common consent among students of mil-

1

itary aviation, only three other carrier fighters
have shared this distinction and proven it in
combat. The first was Japan's elegant little Mitsubishi A6M series, the famed Zero that stunned
Allied fliers in the Pacific during 1941–42. Next
came the Grumman F6F Hellcat, built partly to
combat the Zero and gain air superiority over
invasion beaches. And after the Crusader was
McDonnell's fabulous F-4 Phantom II, which
began life as a fleet defense aircraft and later
became a mainstay of the U.S. Air Force.

In the "honorable mention" category is another Vought product: the F4U Corsair designed by Rex Biesel and Russell Clark. Originally conceived as a carrier fighter, the U-Bird
was a long time in living up to its early promise.
It was at first widely considered unsuitable for
carrier operations and spent the first three years
of its combat life flying almost exclusively from
island bases. Not until the kamikaze crisis of late
1944 were F4Us rushed into squadron-strength
service aboard American flattops. By then the
early problems had been solved, and the bent-
wing bird went on to enhance its already sen-
sational record. The Corsair probably remains
the most versatile single-engine piston-powered
fighter ever flown. Only its teething troubles mar
its superb record as a carrier aircraft.

For Chance Vought, however, things slid
rapidly downhill after the Corsair. Following the
company's move from Connecticut to Texas
after the war, the transition to jet propulsion
brought serious problems. It was a frustrating
period for a company that had been among the
leaders in naval aircraft since the 1920s. But the
fact was, none of the F4U's immediate successors
even began to live up to the Corsair's reputation.
The next three designs were, respectively, a dud,
a dead end, and a disappointment.

First came the radically unconventional

XF5U, which first flew in late 1942. Dubbed "the flying pancake," it was a single flat lifting surface with twin tails and two engines. Intended for vertical flight and high speed, the lone XF5U suffered from inadequate engines during the war. By the time larger powerplants became available, the advent of jet propulsion had rendered the concept obsolete.

Then in 1946, Vought completed its first jet—the single-engine XF6U, christened Pirate in keeping with the firm's nautical lineage. But like many early jets, the F6U was heavy and underpowered. Its 3,000-pound-thrust engine made it slower than late-model Corsairs. Many of the thirty-three Pirates were retroactively fitted with afterburners (the first in the U.S. Navy), but by then other designs were on the boards. The F6U remained a development aircraft, nothing more.

But following the Pirate by two years was Vought's most promising design. On paper the tailless, twin-engine F7U Cutlass looked like a winner—a world-beater in the Corsair mold. The first production bird flew in 1950 and was followed three years later by the F7U-3. This variant was extremely advanced for its time. Designed with afterburning engines, it possessed a maximum level speed of some 700 mph (over 600 knots), and a combat ceiling of 45,000 feet. Not only was the Cutlass the first naval fighter designed with afterburners and swept wings, it was (in the F7U-3M) the first plane armed solely with missiles and the first to release ordnance in excess of Mach 1.

But there were problems, lots of them. The three prototypes were tested at Patuxent River, Maryland, the navy's experimental flight center. Early in the evaluation program, a navy commander met a marine lieutenant colonel who had just landed an XF7U-1.

Two classic Vought fighters: the F7U-3 Cutlass and XF8U-1 Crusader in flight together, January 1956. (U.S. Navy)

"What do you think?" asked the commander. "Is it any good?"

"Nope."

"Well, does it have any potential?"

"Nope."[2]

Though the Cutlass first flew in prototype form in 1948, squadron service had to wait over five years. The test phase, involving "X jobs" and early production birds, was marred by crashes and fatalities. Recalled Boone Guyton, Vought's chief of flight test, "Bill Millar went in at Patuxent River in an XF7U-1. He never recovered, and the actual cause was not ascertained. I, and others, think it was the change-over hydraulic back-up system on the ailerators that we later found—from another fatality at Dallas—could get into a 'twilight zone' and put a 400-pound nose-down pitching force on the elevator."[3]

In all, some 330 F7Us were built. Cutlasses first joined the fleet in April 1954 with VF-81, and operational difficulties quickly arose. The Vought's relatively low climb rate of 13,000 feet per minute gave birth to the nickname "Gutlass." The two Westinghouse J46 engines, each producing 5,800 pounds of thrust in afterburner, could not remedy the situation. In fact, they were part of the problem. One highly experienced navy flier, a combat fighter and test pilot, characterized the F7U as "a gutless, thirsty dog, with low performance and miserable range."[4]

More seriously, the radical fighter suffered an uncommonly high accident rate. So high, in fact, that among new pilots it was called the "Ensign Eliminator." In short, the F7U suffered many of the setbacks experienced by its Corsair predecessor, without the F4U's potential or eventual vindication. The Cutlass remained an unpopular, short-lived aircraft and was retired in November 1957 after only three and a half years in squadron service.

In September of 1952 the navy's Bureau of Aeronautics released specifications for a new fighter. Among the standard carrier requirements—environmental protection, folding wings, and ease of maintenance—was something new. The navy wanted Mach 1 performance. Never before had a shipboard aircraft been expected to exceed the speed of sound in level flight.

Chance Vought, then a division of United Aircraft Corporation, was one of eight manufacturers in contention for the contract. And based upon its recent record, the company's outlook was far from cheerful. The XF5U and F6U had gone nowhere. And the Cutlass, still a new aircraft, was experiencing considerable difficulty. Thus, Vought found itself painted into a corner. There were no contracts pending after the F7U. Old hands around BuAer recall that the bureau chief, Real Admiral Apollo Soucek, laid down the law to the Dallas firm. If the next design wasn't a winner, Vought could kiss the navy goodbye. Apparently the attitude was never officially committed to paper, but it was a very real consideration. J. Russell Clark, long a top Vought engineer, described the F8U program as a "must win" situation.[5]

With that powerful motive well in mind, Russ Clark and his team set out to produce a winner. The field was a fast one, including North American, Douglas, Grumman, and Lockheed. In the next five months a variety of configurations were drafted, considered, rejected, modified, and accepted. With the historical precedent of the Corsair, "Flying Pancake," and Cutlass, there may have been outside expectations of another radical Vought design. But Clark and his associates opted for a conventional configuration enhanced by the availability of new knowledge and technology.

In the early 1950s the navy was wary of swept-wing designs, and not without reason. True, a swept wing allowed high-speed performance—but a carrier aircraft spent the crucial part of its flight profile at low airspeed. Landing aboard ship required positive low-speed control and stability, especially with wheels and flaps down. Thus far, no swept-wing aircraft had joined the fleet.

Nevertheless, in relatively short order Vought decided upon a 42-degree swept wing for the F8U. The competition also included swept-wing designs, as well as a delta and a thin, low-drag straight wing. But Vought's entry was unique in the manner in which it approached the critical low-speed stability problem. A two-position, variable-incidence wing afforded two benefits: it gave the pilot good visibility during takeoff and landing, and, by being raised 7 degrees, allowed for a desirable angle of attack.

Inadequate visibility was one of the F7U's faults. The swept-wing, tailless design necessitated a 20-degree angle of attack on takeoff and landing. This flight attitude severely restricted the pilot's forward vision and required an inordinately long and heavy nose-gear oleo strut. However, the problem was deftly sidestepped in the Crusader. By hinging the wing at the rear spar, only the wing structure was tilted to attain the angle of attack. This tilt was produced through the action of a hydraulic piston. Thus, the pilot's forward view remained largely unaffected and the F8U enjoyed a weight saving with much shorter landing gear.

There were other innovations. Russ Clark described the Crusader as "an outstanding example of integrating high-risk technology, utilizing all 'at the moment' NACA advanced technology, plus Vought's in-house advanced technology." Its features included lightweight wiring; Pratt and Whitney's J57 engine, then rated at 15,000 pounds of thrust; a Marquardt ram air turbine for emergency power; and the new air-conditioning system. All these and more were integrated into the F8U, forming a highly versatile unit.

Advances in metallurgy played a big part in the Crusader's design and construction. At this time materials were catching up with airspeeds, and the F8U was going to be a speedster. The fuselage was composed of 25 percent magnesium alloy while the empennage and part of the center section were titanium—both lightweight, heat-resistant metals. Magnesium had been used in aircraft since World War II, when its exceptionally light weight (only 74 percent greater than water) endeared it to aircraft designers. But in the jet age, magnesium's high melting temperature of 1,472 degrees Fahrenheit assumed even greater importance.

Titanium was then relatively new. It had only been produced on a commercial scale since 1948, but its properties were immediately appreciated. In fact, titanium seemed nature's own refutation of the age-old assertion that if God had meant man to fly, He would have given him wings at birth. For titanium seemed put on earth for the specific purpose of building carrier aircraft. Light and strong, it is virtually rustproof.

7

It is 40 percent lighter than stainless steel, yet offers greater heat resistance. And best of all from the navy's point of view, it is unaffected by saltwater or maritime corrosion. In aircraft construction it frequently fills the gap between light aluminum and heavy steel.

Manufacturing methods were also a consideration in the F8U design. Vought had to find a means of shaping the nose, thinning the aft fuselage with extended afterburner length, and paying close attention to area development theory. The latter involved extensive wind-tunnel tests to perfect the boundary layer, or "Coke bottle" effect, which minimized supersonic drag. Engineers later credited this program with a major role in making possible the Crusader's record-breaking speed.[6]

In short, the F8U was a state-of-the-art aircraft. It brought together the latest knowledge and technology in airframe design, propulsion, and materials. In May 1953, Vought was chosen to build the new fighter—and the navy moved into the era of supersonic flight. In only five months the Dallas team had brought home the one contract it had to have.

That same month a prototype North American F-100 set a world speed record when it became the first operational aircraft to exceed Mach 1 in level flight. The Super Saber was clocked at 755 mph (655 knots), and a new generation of military aircraft had arrived. The F-100 was probably the Crusader's closest air force contemporary. Both were powered by the J57 afterburning engine, but the similarities ended there. The North American weighed about 21,000 pounds empty, while Vought brought in the F8U-1 at 16,500. Thus the Crusader, beneficiary of some bright engineering, reversed the historical advantage in weight comparisons between land-based and carrier-based aircraft.

While the Super Saber was actually a fighter-bomber, equipped for strike missions, the Crusader was a thoroughbred fighter, uncompromised by a multi-mission capability. At the time, the F8U's "stretch" was perhaps unrealized, for it would eventually prove a versatile design. But for the near future, it was armed solely for aerial combat, with four 20-mm cannon, two Sidewinder heat-seeking missiles, and thirty-two internally-mounted 2.75-inch rockets.

Ruggedness and simplicity were designed into the Crusader. It was built low to the ground, allowing relative ease of access by maintenance crews. And no control surfaces were installed outboard on the wings, where ailerons usually went. Instead, they were kept inboard of the wing-fold line, so that control linkages would remain less complex. The small flaps, made of magnesium, were positioned immediately next to the fuselage, but when retracted, merged with the aluminum droop ailerons. But while the F8U's wing was a complex unit, it was enormously functional and strong. The airframe as a whole was rated at 6.4 Gs positive and 3.0 Gs negative, the "official" figures in the pilots' manuals.[7]

Actually, as every aviator knew, the published figures included a "fudge factor" as a safety measure. The factors determining stress level on an airframe include aircraft weight, airspeed, and altitude as well as maneuvering forces. Thus, an aircraft could exceed its design limit by 10 percent regularly, or 20 percent occasionally, and return home intact. Military requirements required that an airframe be tested statically to one and a half times the design limit, and in the Crusader this amounted to plus 9.6 and minus 4.5 Gs.

Among other thin-wing fighters of the time, less tolerance existed between design and maximum-stress levels. Wing flexing was ever-

9

present in turbulent air, and high G loads caused visible bends. For example, F-86 pilots had to anticipate flexing while pulling Gs because the wingtips would bend, thus losing the angle of attack. This induced a nose-up pitching motion that could stress the aircraft beyond tolerance. But as one flying admiral recalled, the F8U-1 had "a nice springy gait because it flexed so harmoniously." Therefore, it took close to eight bending Gs to permanently deform (if not disintegrate) a Crusader.[8]

In June 1953 all the engineering and test data were put to practical use when BuAer ordered two XF8U-1s. Work proceeded apace, including over 500 hours of simulator time, and in twenty-one months the first Crusader was ready to fly. It was an impressive performance for Vought, just as impressive as the five-month design period. In March 1955 the prototype was loaded aboard an air force C-124 transport at Dallas and taken to Edwards Air Force Base near

Vought test pilot John Konrad, who made the first flights in most Crusader models. (Vought)

Lancaster, California. Edwards was the best-equipped test facility in the nation, with all the room imaginable in the high desert. On 25 March, the Vought team was set to go.

The one word that characterized the company's attitude toward the Crusader was *confidence*. So certain of the bird was the design team that it formulated an unheard-of plan for the maiden flight. The XF8U-1 would try to exceed Mach 1—on its very first flight. Such an ambitious goal had probably never been set for an untried aircraft, but Russ Clark, his engineers, and the test pilot were willing to try.

The man behind the stick was John W. Konrad, an experienced air force test pilot and Vought's chief of flight test. He started the J57, taxied onto the dry lake bed, checked his instruments, and advanced the throttle. The needle-nosed fighter boomed off the concrete-hard earth and accelerated away. Fifty-two minutes later Konrad was safely back, with the first flight and supersonic speed both in the bag. In fact, he had tickled the 1.1 figure on the Mach meter, with no apparent difficulty. In debriefing, Konrad said that acceleration through the sonic barrier was "smooth, pleasant, and rapid."[9] Konrad would make the first flight in all Crusader models over the next six years except for the F8U-2 and the French version. (Vought personnel joked that he was anxious to collect the bonus money for first flights in new models.)

From spring through fall of 1955, company test pilots explored the Crusader's performance. It was a busy program, even with the completion of a second prototype, as the number-one bird logged one hundred flights in those six months. Cameras and telemetry equipment provided a continuing source of data for engineers to examine. Probably the most important discovery in the early flights was the Crusader's crabbing motion at high altitude. This yawing tendency

11

was cured by adding a pair of ventral fins to later versions of the F8U-2 and all subsequent models.

Another change in the F8U-2 was the ejection seat. Originally Vought had installed a seat of its own, but for purposes of standardization the seat became GFE—government-furnished equipment. By this time the navy had settled on the British-designed Martin-Baker series, which had proved its worth thousands of times around the world. Originally used in the Royal Air Force, Martin-Bakers eventually were found in a wide variety of military aircraft, saving aviators from death at nearly all altitudes and airspeeds.

The situations in which Martin-Bakers were employed included attempted underwater ejections. Usually, a carrier plane takes its pilot into the water during a failed catapult shot. If the pilot is really sharp, he can punch out before he hits the water—but he needs cat-quick reflexes. More often than not, he rides his aircraft into the sea and departs with an awesome splash of finality.

Of four known underwater ejection attempts in F-8s, two were successful. The first unsuccessful incident occurred in 1962 when an F8U-1 went down, and the pilot was listed as lost at sea. Seven years later his remains, and some wreckage that indicated he had attempted a sub-surface ejection, were recovered.

In 1965 an F-8E took a "cold cat shot" in which the catapult failed. The Crusader went into the water nose-down, but the impact was moderate. The aviator tried to blow his canopy, but it only moved a few inches. However, this allowed water to enter the cockpit, approximately equalizing the pressure, and the lucky flier ejected underwater with only minor injuries.

Two years later another E model went into the water during a night launch. Pulling his face

An early production F8U-1 taxiing with its variable-incidence wing in the raised position. Note absence of refueling probe, fuselage missile rails, large ventral fins, and underwing stores—all were added to later Crusaders. (Vought)

curtain, the pilot ejected through the canopy. The seat fell away and the pilot inflated his life vest, but he found himself pulled down by his parachute, which had snagged on the doomed Crusader. Though badly hurt, the aviator held his breath long enough to work free and rise to the surface. He was rescued by a helicopter.

The fourth known attempt was technically a failed ejection, but the pilot survived. An F-8J pilot in 1969 tried three times to eject, without success. In desperation he hit the ditching handle, which popped the canopy and disconnected his personal equipment console. He swam free to the surface.

The Vought-supplied ejection seats did their share of work in the F8U program, but the Crusader's test-and-development losses were half the F7U's. In all, five F8Us were destroyed while being evaluated by company or military pilots, but three of the aviators survived. The two fatalities both occurred during high-speed tests—one the result of materiel failure, the other induced unintentionally.

After John Konrad's first flight, tests continued at Edwards, and in February 1956 Harry Brackett was engaged in a series of speed runs. During one such pass, an aileron broke loose, causing a rapid sequence of damage that tore

13

the aircraft apart. In split seconds, the F8U-1 disintegrated; Brackett never had a chance to eject.

Three months later, on 4 May, marine Captain James Feliton had to eject from his "dash one" during navy evaluation tests. Then, in mid-August, John Konrad found himself with a dead engine at high altitude. Despite repeated attempts, he could not manage an air start, so he rang up the "for sale" sign.

The second fatality occurred in June of 1957 when Vought hosted a class from the Navy Post-Graduate School. Test pilot Jim Buckner provided the officers with a look at the Crusader in flight, but they witnessed more than anyone intended. Buckner, no doubt conscious of the impression he could make at the home drome, screamed across the ramp in front of the company's control tower. In an abrupt pull-up, he exceeded the airframe's tolerance and suffered a structural failure. Like Harry Brackett sixteen months before, he had no time to get out.

Later, when the French Navy ordered F8U-2NEs, which became F-8E (FN)s, big Bob Rostine tested one of the prototypes. He got into a stalled configuration from which he was unable to recover, and safely ejected. Both Konrad and Rostine were involved in other close calls in which their planes were damaged, but they landed intact. Konrad had control-system failure in an early photo bird during a 1957 flight. Rostine, in March 1958, was testing a "dash one" with an experimental leading edge for the XF8U-3. At a high angle of attack, with the new leading edge jammed downward, the Crusader slammed into the ground on landing and sheared off its wheels.

As Vought and the navy acquired experience, the main-gear legs were identified as a continuing source of trouble. The hydraulic accumulator atop the shock strut failed in several

F8U-1s, most often during carrier landings. In most instances they were normal traps, but "normal" is a relative term since navy pilots have long called deck landings "controlled crashes." However, most Crusaders damaged in this fashion were repairable. Dragging speed brakes were another cause of damage, even without landing-gear trouble, often owing to partial loss of hydraulic pressure through leaking seals.

While the test phase continued, production moved ahead. The first flight of a production F8U-1 came in September 1955. In late 1957 Chance Vought was awarded a $200 million contract for more "dash ones," and a total of 318 F8U-1s were built. A nearly identical variant was the -1E, incorporating the AN/APS-67 fire-control radar, which replaced the APG-30 system in the original Crusader. One hundred thirty -1Es were produced. (Another model was also then forthcoming—the F8U-1P, of which 144 were built. These photo aircraft were vastly different internally from the "straight dash ones" and

F8U-1s of VF-32, the first fleet squadron to receive Crusaders. The Swordsmen made the first Atlantic Fleet F8U deployment aboard Saratoga *(CVA 60) in February 1958, the same month VF-154 introduced the type to Pacific operations aboard* Hancock *(CVA 19). (Peter B. Mersky)*

-1Es, and are thus dealt with separately in chapter 4.)

Approximately the first fifty F8U-1s were delivered without an in-flight refueling capability. But from then on, a refueling probe was standard equipment. It was retractable within an elliptical blister portside, aft of the cockpit in the fighters. (On photo aircraft, the probe was flush mounted.)

Next in sequence came 187 F8U-2s. The Martin-Baker ejection seats were installed, and the Pratt and Whitney J57-P-16 was used, providing 500 pounds of additional thrust, with air intakes added to cool the afterburner area. Piloted by Jim Omvig, the "dash two" first flew in August 1958, and preliminary evaluation was completed late that year.

In the late 1950s and early 1960s the navy and marines still operated special-purpose night fighters, and 152 Crusaders were built for this mission. These were designated F8U-2Ns, and orders for them amounted to nearly $100 million in 1959. An infrared scanner was installed ahead of the windscreen, augmenting the improved radar-tracking–fire-control unit. An autopilot was standard in the -2N, and propulsion was again upped, by 700 pounds, in the J57-P-20. Offsetting the weight of the additional avionics and equipment was the deletion of the rocket pack, and no further Crusaders retained this original armament feature. John Konrad logged the new fighter's first flight in February 1960.

Finally came 286 F8U-2NEs. Diverted from the original pure fighter concept, these aircraft were built with two wing pylons to carry external ordnance: bombs, missiles, and air-to-ground rockets. They also featured a larger radar dish, which required a rounded nose cone. (The French Navy models incorporated boundary-layer control and advanced wing leading edges, but the 42 F-8E(FN)s will be dealt with separately.)

Including the two prototypes, total U.S. Navy and Marine construction of the Crusader came to 1,219 aircraft. Of the two main variants, "dash twos" accounted for about 51 percent. Construction ended in January 1965 with the final French aircraft, but Vought was kept busy with a lengthy remanufacturing program. This was a four-year project destined to update worthwhile examples of all Crusader models except the 318 F8U-1s. Eventually 446 aircraft were rebuilt or extensively modified between 1966 and 1970. The changes primarily involved new wings and center sections, A-7A-type main-gear struts, advanced electronics, and increased payload capacity.

The XF8U-1, when designed in 1953–54, had no specific airframe fatigue life. Instead, the usual static strength criteria were employed, with attention to good detail design. Vought estimated that the average Crusader would operate with the fleet for seven years.

Then in 1956 the navy decided to determine specific fatigue-life criteria for modern fighter aircraft. Developed as the BuAer Design Spectrum, the criteria included the number of flight hours and the number and magnitude of stress loads that any single airplane might encounter in its career. By 1958 the Spectrum for the Crusader was established at 2,000 hours, including Modification Change ECP401, which brought existing F8Us up to that standard.[10]

The Vietnam War, however, considerably accelerated the Crusader's rate of flight hours. Naturally, this resulted in an equal reduction in the "life" remaining in active aircraft. With a large portion of the F-8 population approaching or exceeding the 2,000-hour mark, the inventory was being eroded faster than normal.

17

Therefore, in 1966 the remanufacture program was initiated. In the four years during which the redesignated F-8H, J, K, and L models were rebuilt, their service life became twice the original. When returned to the navy from Dallas, the Hotel through Lima F-8s were good for another 4,000 hours.

Production is perhaps the most neglected aspect of aviation history, but it was a notable part of the Crusader story. Vought built eight F8Us per month, though facilities existed for a rollout rate of five times as many. But since the entire production run was conducted in peacetime, full use of factory potential was unnecessary.

By the end of 1959, over 500 Crusaders had been delivered. By mid-1961 the total was nearly 1,000, bringing Chance Vought something over $1 billion in six years. However, some idea of the navy's attitude towards the Crusader may be gained by a comparison of the number of early jet fighters it ordered.

The early navy jets were aptly described by Tom Wolfe as "a delirium of sharp teeth, cold steel, cosmic warlords, and evil spirits."[11] There were Cougars, Cutlasses, Skyknights, and Demons. The first two carrier jets were McDonnell's FH-1 and the North American FJ-1, both delivered to the fleet in 1947. Between them, the Phantom I and the Fury totaled fewer than a hundred aircraft. But "Mr. Mac" sold nearly 900 F2H-1 through -4 Banshees—big, robust, twin-engine planes that remained in service for a decade.

Grumman's initial batch of F9F-2s arrived in 1949, and the Korean War ensured that the "dash three" through "five" models were kept in demand. Well over 1,300 Panthers were built, remaining active until 1958. Then the sweptwing F9F-6 through -8 added 2,000 more to the inventory. In short, over 3,300 F9Fs were deliv-

ered to the navy and marines. No other jet fighter has come close to this record in U.S. naval service.

In the early to mid-1950s, six more fighter types entered fleet squadrons, excluding the Crusader. North American's updated Fury, the FJ-2 through -4, made a sizeable impression with some 1,100 in service from 1954 to 1962. But none of the others amounted to half the Fury's number. These ranged from 201 F11F-1 Tigers to 519 of the impressive, racy-looking F3H-1 and -2 Demons.

Therefore, the Crusader was built in larger numbers than any navy jet up to its time with the exception of the F9F family. Since then the F-4 Phantom II has topped the 5,000 mark for all services worldwide, but the F8U still retains a respectable place in the "numbers game" of U.S. Navy aircraft.

The Phantom indirectly caused a change in aircraft designations for the U.S. armed forces, and of course the Crusader was affected. By the time Vought's "reman" program got under way, the change already had occurred. It came in Sep-

The Crusader was one of the first Navy aircraft with an in-flight refueling capability. Here an F8U-1P receives fuel from an A4D-2 with "buddy pack" underwing tanks. Photo Crusaders' fuel probes were mounted flush with the fuselage, unlike fighters, which had a bulge over the probe. (Peter B. Mersky)

19

tember of 1962, apparently under peculiar circumstances. At least two Pentagon insiders attribute the unpopular action to Secretary of Defense Robert S. McNamara's inability to keep the air force and navy systems separate. The story goes that McNamara embarrassed himself before a congressional panel by referring to the Phantom as two aircraft. It was a new type at the time, with barely two years of squadron service. The navy, original customer of the Phantom, called it the F4H-1 (later F-4A). When the air force adopted the Phantom that year, it was designated F-110 and entered production as the F-4C. Apparently McNamara, confused by the manufacturer's identifier (H for McDonnell) under the navy system, thought he was talking about two separate designs: the incomplete navy F4H and the complete air force F-4C designations. So an interservice aircraft-designation system was adopted to alleviate any future confusion.

Thus, the entire Crusader clan was renamed. F8U-1s became F-8As; -1Es became F-8Bs, and so on. Then things were further complicated when remanufactured F-8 Bravos were returned to the fleet as Limas, and F8Cs (out of sequence) as Ks. The upshot was that hundreds of Crusaders bore three designations during their careers. Most naval aviators took it in stride with a minimal amount of complaint, seeming to adopt a "good enough for government work" attitude. But there were a few traditionalists who mourned the passing of a system they'd known all their lives.

Joining the Fleet

2

The Crusader did all that its Corsair ancestor had done for the navy fighter community, and perhaps more. While the F4U had muscled in on Grumman's monopoly of carrier fighters, the F8U established quite a record of its own. The F9F series far outnumbered other navy fighters of the time, but an early taste of the Vought set many Grumman partisans on edge.

Perhaps the earliest episode occurred when Commander R. W. "Duke" Windsor, a sandy-haired test pilot, delivered the first production F8U-1 from Dallas to Patuxent River. One of Windsor's close friends in the business was Ralph Clark, a Grumman technical service representative. The test pilot phoned Clark and said, in so many words, "You guys are in trouble. This airplane is a winner."[1]

Indeed it was. Vought had guaranteed a top speed of Mach 1.4, but at no extra cost the Crusader proved capable of 1.7, and a bit more. By way of comparison, the early F11F Tiger, with Wright's J65 engine, was rated at 1.2.

The Crusader underwent as thorough an evaluation as any aircraft produced in its time, but with minimal delay. In barely a year, flight test and engineering experiments were conducted; then the F8U entered the final phase of operational testing. For a carrier aircraft, of course, that meant "hitting the boat."

Initial carrier qualifications (car-quals) were made during April 1956. The pilot was Duke Windsor, who flew the fourth pre-production aircraft, BuAer 140446. Between 20 and 30 March, Windsor made seventy-six field carrier landings, directed by both a mirror landing system and an LSO. The F8U-1 went aboard the USS *Forrestal* at Norfolk, Virginia, on 3 April, accompanied by Windsor and a Vought contingent led by Russ Clark. The Pax River pilot made six touch-and-go landings to get a feel for the Crusader's deck-handling qualities, then tests began in earnest on the 4th.

At the time of his first F8U catapult shot, Windsor had logged thirty-eight flights in the test aircraft for a total of thirty-six hours. During 4 and 5 April he made twelve cat shots and twelve landings, all normal with one noteworthy exception.

The fifth launch was to be made with full afterburner. However, NATC's catapult crew installed the wrong holdback, as F3Hs, F11Fs, and A3Ds were also aboard. When Windsor lit the burner, his Crusader slewed down the deck and he immediately knew something was wrong. Quickly throttling back to idle power, he jumped on the brakes, locked them as much as possible, then retarded throttle to idle-cutoff. The errant Crusader lurched to a stop, four feet from the bow. Amid considerable activity and not a little cursing from the cat crew, Windsor looked up at the navigation bridge where Russ Clark had almost seen his pride and joy plunge overboard. Duke gave the engineer a thumbs up, indicating no damage, and tests resumed without further incident. A second sea period during 18 and 19 April involved eleven more arrested landings and a dozen launches.

Two months later, Windsor and marine Captain Jim Feliton conducted *Essex*-class carquals aboard the *Bon Homme Richard* out of San Diego. On the tenth landing, Feliton sustained a main-gear fracture, spewing hydraulic fluid in all directions. But the Crusader escaped damage, and the new Vought was considered carrier-qualified. Through these tests, the F8U demonstrated exceptional stability on launch. Later, a fleet pilot would describe the U-Bird as "a joy on the catapult shot."[2] It accelerated to 180 knots in about two seconds from 210 feet of catapult. The F8U became airborne nearly hands-off, thanks to the incidence of the raised wing.

In fleet service, the Crusader most frequently flew from modified *Essex*-class ships. These 27,000-ton vessels, mostly built during World War II, offered relatively little margin for error compared to the vastly larger *Forrestals*. Pilots soon discovered that landing an F8U aboard a "27 Charlie" conversion required skill and precision.

Basically, the problem involved a high approach speed (147 knots at maximum landing weight) and a small deck. Actual touchdown speed was less, but the *Essex* class offered only 10 feet or so of hook-to-ramp clearance. It was easy to misjudge the approach and hit the stern edge of the flight deck. In fact, Air Wing 21 aboard the *Hancock* recorded fourteen ramp strikes on its 1966–67 cruise, involving everything from tail hooks to whole airplanes.[3]

Compounding the situation was "a miserable power curve."[4] In landing configuration, the Crusader's power curve was hardly a curve at all—it more resembled a flat line on the graph. The pilot had a 12-knot interval in which the required power only varied about 1 percent. Hence, it was terribly easy to get into trouble. Here's how it happened:

At optimum angle of attack for landing, the

wing was raised 7 degrees, further increased in camber by an automatic interconnect that drooped the leading edge 25 degrees and lowered the ailerons a similar amount. This was a carefully designed system that enhanced low-speed stability and control on landing approach.

Nevertheless, in this configuration the aircraft could decelerate about 10 knots—very near the stall—without the pilot becoming aware of an underpowered situation. At the point the feedback of variable power requirements was inadequate to overcome the increasing drag.

As airspeed lowered imperceptibly, drag increased and the Crusader began to settle. Now the pilot became aware of the problem. He added power and invariably raised the nose, which only compounded the drag and bled off airspeed. The F8U was now in a classically perilous situation. As drag increased further and the aircraft continued to lose height, the pilot continued milking back on the stick, attempting to solve his problem with stabilator instead of throttle.

The correct procedure was frequently applied too late. On the charted power curve, airspeed was now to the left of the line showing power required to overcome drag. Once this spot was reached, the situation became irretrievable. The Crusader was now decelerating faster than application of full power could counter, and there was nowhere to go but down.

And this entire sequence occurred in something under three seconds.

Therefore, pilots had to monitor their airspeed constantly, or end up on the carrier's ramp—or in the water. At night, of course, the problem was compounded. Without reference to the horizon to catch minute attitude changes, which almost instantly became airspeed changes, the aviator had nothing to relate to control-stick inputs. Under these circumstances, the situation could rapidly get out of hand.

Fortunately, a technical solution did exist. The auto-throttle, sensitive to changes in attitude and airspeed on landing, automatically compensated and kept the Crusader at the proper power setting. Power control was so crucial—especially in night carrier landings—that in most F8U squadrons, an inoperable auto-throttle was cause to abort a nocturnal flight.

After a while, F8U pilots found a simpler solution to their problem. They cut off the right thumb of their gloves to gain maximum control of the cone-shaped "coolie hat" trim buttons on their control sticks. By employing the sensitive flexing portion of their thumbs, they gained better attitude control during the crucial phase of landing, by trimming nose up or down as required. Soon the thumbless gloves became a trademark of the Crusader community. Some aviators went so far as to cut off all the fingers, giving their nomex gloves the appearance of a set of European driving gloves.

Another notorious feature of the Crusader was its stall-spin characteristics. But it was an "honest" aircraft, giving ample warning of the stall that could lead to a violent, pitching spin. Lieutenant Norm Gandia, an instructor pilot in VF-174, insisted that one had to be a ham-fisted ignoramus to spin the bird.

In August of 1965, Gandia was the bogie in a two-on-one ACM flight. The student wingman was pitched out of the fight, which became one-on-one between Gandia and the element leader. Finally the two instructors found themselves abreast of one another at 11,000 feet, doing something under 150 knots. Gandia turned into his opponent and, losing flying speed, felt the Crusader depart. He was in a right-hand spin.

25

Standard procedure called for a pilot to eject if still spinning at 10,000 feet, since the F-8's fully developed spin rate cost 1,500 feet per turn. But Gandia had stalled at 11,000, so by the completion of the first evolution he was below "safe" altitude. However, he determined to stay with the airplane, preferring to ride it down rather than walk back and have his students remind him of the mentality involved in spinning an F-8 to begin with!

Gandia reached down, unlocked and raised the variable-incidence wing. He also pushed full forward stick and booted full left rudder. The spin became progressively more violent, with faster rotation and jarring pitch-ups. The other instructor followed Gandia down, screaming for him to eject. But Norm Gandia was a stubborn fighter pilot. He stayed with it.

At about the sixth turn, with the nose well down, Gandia stopped the spin. But he was then below 2,000 feet and his nose was pointed straight down. It was going to be awfully close. By the time he pulled into level flight, there was about 100 feet of air between him and the Atlantic Ocean.

The navy accepted its first F8U-1s on 28 December 1956. The early deliveries were allotted to various bases for further operational testing, and among the first recipients was Developmental Squadron Three at Atlantic City, New Jersey. Previously this job had been performed by Tactical Test at Patuxent River, but now VX-3 had the responsibility.

Six VX squadrons existed in the navy at this time. VX-1, for instance, worked with new antisubmarine aircraft; VX-5 evaluated attack planes. The skipper of VX-3 was Captain Robert G. Dosé, a big, enthusiastic aviator who had worn Wings of Gold since 1936. Most of his career had been spent in fighters, and he was no stranger to Vought aircraft. Dosé had been exec of the navy's first F4U squadron when Commander Joe Clifton formed VF-12 in 1942.

Prior to receiving its initial F8Us, VX-3 had tested a variety of early jet fighters—most notably, the North American FJ Fury, the Douglas F4D, and McDonnell's futuristic F3H Demon. Atlantic City's first Crusader was the seventeenth production bird, eventually followed by six more "dash ones," and two or three replacements.[5]

Bob Dosé, in his second year as CO of VX-3, immediately took to the Crusader. Of the jets he had flown to date, he considered the F8U "the most spectacular performer." Early in the evaluation program he tested the time-to-climb capability, and was suitably impressed. From brakes off to 40,000 feet took only two and a half minutes. Recalled Dosé, "If you looked back over your shoulder at 40,000 you could see the field below your tail. That's how steep we could climb—about 70 degrees."[6]

Atlantic City performed a variety of tests with its F8U-1s, including weapons evaluation. Naturally, the fighter mission appealed to most VX-3 pilots, and they welcomed the opportunity to tangle with local air force squadrons. On 30 January 1957, Bob Dosé was leading a supersonic formation flight at 43,000 feet when he spotted two Lockheed F-94s below him. As a senior officer, Dosé was supposed to be above such things, but he yielded to temptation. The CO led a bounce on the Starfires, then pulled up in a wingover 10,000 feet above them.

Dosé was just congratulating himself for being the luckiest four-striper in the U.S. Navy when he heard a sharp noise and felt a tremor in his Crusader. His engine had exploded, apparently from faulty fuel metering.

"Your mind works kind of funny at times

27

like those," Dosé reflected later. "I distinctly remember thinking to myself that those air force pilots would be saying, 'Serves him right!' "[7]

Dosé levelled off and glided at 250 knots across New Jersey, heading east. He tried six air starts, as the engine idled at 21 percent power. He got it up to 28 percent but the J57 refused to catch. Finally over the coast, Dosé had no choice but to eject. Dressed in a cotton flight suit, he was ill-prepared for a dunking in the winter Atlantic. But efficient rescue work by an SA-16 amphibian effected a pickup eleven minutes after the CO hit the water. Still, he caught a bad chill and sneezed for an hour. This episode earned Bob Dosé the dubious distinction of probably being the only captain to make an emergency bailout from a jet aircraft.

Meanwhile, Crusaders were going directly to the navy. On 21 March 1957, F8U-1s arrived straight from Dallas without intermediate inspections, the first time such a delivery was made. From then on, however, such a procedure became largely standard. Then four days later the Swordsmen of VF-32 became the first Crusader squadron in the fleet when its initial batch of "dash ones" arrived. It was exactly two years since John Konrad's first flight in the prototype—a record for delivery of a new jet aircraft.

Fighting 32, under Commander G. C. Buhrer, was based at Cecil Field, Florida. The squadron had received the first F9F-6s, the swept-wing Cougars, in November 1952, but the Crusader was a wholly new design. As such, it was phased into the squadron under a controlled atmosphere. Commander Buhrer took some of his pilots, in company with a few from VF(AW)-3, to Patuxent River before squadron delivery. This procedure allowed the aviators to ask questions, poke and probe, and feel out the new birds before they went operational. Following his

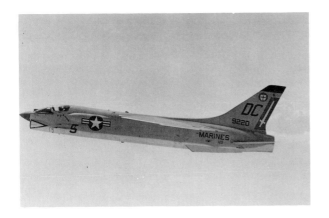

Among early Marine Crusader squadrons was VMF-122 which, as the markings indicate, called itself the Crusaders. This F8U-2NE was based at MCAS Cherry Point, North Carolina, in 1962. (U.S. Marine Corps)

checkout in the F8U, Buhrer spoke for most new Crusader pilots: "It's tremendous."[8]

The marines received their first F8Us before year-end. In December 1957, VMF(AW)-122 transitioned from FJ-3s to F8U-1s. Appropriately, 122 called itself the Crusaders, and the squadron's shield insignia with a crusader's cross became part of F8U heraldry.

The pace now quickened. Crusaders deployed for their first cruises in February 1958. In the Pacific, the VF-154 Black Knights went aboard the *Hancock* while VF-32 rode the *Saratoga* to the Mediterranean. At first, the Swordsmen participated in Sixth Fleet maneuvers, but a few months later they were engaged in more serious work. During the year, an opposition movement had developed within Lebanon that threatened the pro-Western government of President Camille Chamoun. In July the opposition erupted into open revolt, and Chamoun requested that President Eisenhower provide military assistance. Marines were put ashore, and Sixth Fleet carriers stood by to provide air support, if necessary.

Saratoga aircraft were assigned standing patrols during the two-month crisis, and VF-32 was as deeply involved as any squadron. The F8U-

29

1s logged 533 hours during July and 762 more up to 23 August. At that time the situation eased, and American involvement ashore ended with the formation of a new government. The *Forrestal* arrived to relieve "Sara" on station, but Crusaders remained active. New F8U-2s of a marine squadron, VMF-333, were embarked in the *Forrestal* and helped maintain an American presence.

When the Lebanese crisis occurred, the navy was anxious to rush additional aircraft to the Med. The *Saratoga* and *Essex* were reinforced during the operation with more F8Us from the East Coast of the United States. The Crusaders flew via the Azores and Lyautey, Morocco, before recovering aboard the carriers. This procedure had been pioneered in May of that year when eight East Coast fighters flew to the Mediterranean in Operation Pipeline. Four F8Us and four F3H Demons made a nonstop transatlantic crossing on 17 May as a practical test for bolstering Sixth Fleet defenses.

The Crusader now began to settle down to routine duty in the fleet, particularly in the Med. Those were the days when American politicians and military careerists basked in a confidence that seems worlds removed from the grim reality of the 1980s. The "middle sea" was in reality an American lake, and some of the more vocal pundits smugly concluded, "The Russian bear doesn't like to get its feet wet." Of course, that was before the bear developed a fondness for swimming.

Crusaders allowed new techniques for air combat and fleet defense. Air Group Ten aboard the *Forrestal* experimented with operational procedures in the Mediterranean, including VF-103 with its new F8U-1s. The CO was Lieutenant Commander Marvin P. South, a "mustang" who had been commissioned from the ranks. Highly popular with his troops, Mike South was known as a pilot's pilot. He was also popular with Vice Admiral "Cat" Brown, ComSixthFleet.

During Allied exercises in the Med, Brown became disgruntled with the ease and relative impunity with which Royal Air Force bombers out of Malta "sank" his ships. High-flying Canberras came over the carriers at extreme altitude, above effective interception range, and "bombed" to their hearts' delight. Then the Crusaders joined the Sixth Fleet. Admiral Brown dispatched the Sluggers of VF-103 and was pleased with the feedback from his British colleagues. The Crusader came as a considerable surprise when South's pilots began making vertical passes at the Canberras.

Fleet pilots were equally enthusiastic about the F8U's dogfighting potential. Said Lieutenant Woody Cater of VF-103, "It was fantastic. You could fight with the nose above the horizon. In

The shamrock-marked F8U-2s of VMF-333 aboard USS Forrestal *operated in the Mediterranean during the Lebanon crisis of 1958. (U.S. Marine Corps)*

the F9F at 35,000 feet, you had to drop the nose if you put any Gs on the aircraft. In the F8U, we pulled full G loads."[9]

The afterburning J57 engine not only gave the Crusader vertical performance, but acceleration as well. It was a new dimension in fighter aviation. For instance, the F8U-2N's combat weight was 25,000 pounds with 18,000 pounds of thrust—a thrust-to-weight ratio of .71 to one. Grumman's F9F-8 Cougar had a thrust-to-weight ratio of .41 to one.

The Crusader possessed similar advantages over the navy's other jets. Prior to the F8U, the two most popular carrier fighters were the FJ-3 Fury and F2H Banshee series, though they were vastly different aircraft. North American's Fury was more like a sports car, while the Banshee resembled a Cadillac. But like all jets of the late 1940s to mid-1950s, they lacked high-altitude performance. In the year before the F8U reached the fleet, three other carrier fighters became operational: two interceptors and a pure fighter. These were, respectively, the F3H Demon and F4D Skyray, plus Grumman's F11F Tiger. The latter was delivered the same month as the Crusader, intended as insurance against the possibility of a Vought failure. The Tiger was a nimble little dogfighter, but the F8U's success rendered it unnecessary. Only 201 were built. Similarly, the F3H and F4D were limited to 520 and 420 examples each.

The first F8U-2 squadron was VF-84, the Jolly Rogers, which became operational in April of 1959. By then a genuine depth of experience existed in the fleet, and the Crusader was fully established. It was officially rated at Mach 1.7, though pilots could and did push it within a shade of Mach 2. As of 1960, over half the navy's thirty carrier-based fighter squadrons and most marine fighter units flew Crusaders. Detachments of F8U-1Ps were aboard all attack carriers to provide light photo reconnaissance while three marine recce squadrons also flew -1Ps.

Crusaders began the new year of 1962 in impressive fashion, which was appropriate as it would be the most important year to date for the Vought. On 17 January, the F8U helped inaugurate a new era in naval aviation as Commander George C. Talley orbited the new carrier *Enterprise*, at sea off Norfolk, Virginia. Inheritor of one of the greatest names in U.S. Navy history, the "Big E" was the world's first nuclear-powered aircraft carrier.

When the snow had finally been plowed off the deck, Talley dropped into the groove and logged the first trap aboard the *Enterprise*. Fighting 62, the Boomerang squadron, flew its Crusaders with Talley's Air Group One on the supercarrier's shakedown cruise to the Caribbean. Air Wing Six then became the Big E's regular operational unit until late 1964, including F8U-2NEs and F-8Es of VF-33, plus detachments of VFP-62.

Also in January, the first transpacific crossing by a marine jet fighter squadron took place. Lieutenant Colonel Charles E. Crew, skipper of VMF(AW)-451, led eighteen F8U-2Ns from MCAS El Toro, California, to Atsugi, Japan. The Crusader nightfighters hopped "across the pond" with refueling stops at Kaneohe, Hawaii, Wake Island, and Guam. In-flight refueling was also accomplished along the way. Like many Texas gals, the Crusader had long, limber legs.

In the early 1960s, navy and marine F8Us were flying upwards of 15,000 hours per month. But one month in particular would be remembered by Crusader photo pilots. And the world.

The weekend of 13-14 October 1962 started like any other for the personnel of VFP-62 at NAS Cecil Field near Jacksonville, Florida. Some had planned trips, others anticipated family outings or a lazy two days at home. Then, abruptly,

33

Light Photo Squadron 62, based at NAS Jacksonville, Florida, provided most of the low-level reconnaissance of Cuba after Soviet missiles were discovered there in October 1962. (U.S. Navy)

things began to change. The squadron was ordered to provide a regular duty section and a stand-by section. Personal travel was restricted to within 50 miles of Jacksonville.

Russian missiles had been reported in Cuba.

When the crisis broke, "Fightin' Photo" 62 had two detachments aboard Sixth Fleet carriers. Two more dets were hastily ordered to flattops in the Caribbean. The squadron CO, Commander W. B. Ecker, barely had time to get these latter units off the ground. One of them was detailed to a carrier with only two hours notice.

The importance of photo coverage of Cuba went beyond the basic military need for intelligence. President Kennedy needed proof that the Soviets were in fact moving strategic weapons into the Western Hemisphere, and photos were the best means of demonstrating that chilling

Assisting in photo coverage of Cuba during the missile crisis of October 1962 was VMCJ-2, which sent five of its six RF-8As to help VFP-62 at NAS Jacksonville and Key West, Florida. (U.S. Marine Corps)

fact to the world. Therefore, VFP-62 became one of the most important elements of national policy. It was the only unit capable of gathering adequate low-level photos of Cuba in the time required.

Ecker, however, was extremely short-handed. After the four detachments left Jacksonville, he needed more planes and pilots. And, in legendary fashion, the marines landed—literally—in the nick of time.

Marine Composite Photo Squadron Two at MCAS Cherry Point, North Carolina, was the source of Ecker's reinforcements. Five pilots were quickly detached to VFP-62. They had to wait while new navy high-speed cameras were installed in their RF-8As (designations had changed the month before), then sped south to Jacksonville. There Ecker routed Crusaders to NAS Key West, the jump-off point for flights over Cuba. Key West, only about 100 miles north-northwest of Havana, gave the RF-8s excellent position to cover all of Cuba. Photo flights began on Monday the 15th.

Air Force U-2s had uncovered the first evidence of Soviet missiles in Cuba. But one of the high-flying spy planes was knocked down by a surface-to-air missile, the pilot killed. Subsequent photo coverage of the island was therefore

35

conducted at lower altitude. The navy and marine pilots began flying at treetop level on the 23rd, and that remained their technique for the balance of the operation.

The "Blue Moon" flights imposed a heavy schedule on everyone involved. Two flights a day were flown out of Key West, in varying strength. Four of the five marines and six VFP-62 pilots made repeated low-level dashes over Castro's domain, most often in pairs. One of the marines, Captain R. C. Conway, described the tactics: "The whole idea was to come in fast and low, barely over the water, then quickly pull up to the desired altitude for the cameras when we reached the shoreline. After that, it was max speed over the island, and look out for the mountain tops!"[10]

Upon landing at Key West, the Crusaders' cameras were unloaded and their film packs

In addition to flying reconnaissance missions from Florida, VFP-62 also sent detachments to sea during the missile crisis. This RF-8A prepared to launch from USS Independence, *steaming in the Caribbean. (Vought)*

flown to VFP-62's photo lab at Cecil Field. Once the prints were developed, they were rushed to Washington for interpretation and analysis. Thus, in a matter of a few hours, President Kennedy or U.N. Ambassador Adlai Stevenson could examine the photos and show the world what the Russians were up to in the Caribbean.

In all, VFP-62 and its VMCJ-2 "loaners" flew over eighty sorties in a six-week period, amounting to 100-plus hours of surveillance. The RF-8s brought back some 160,000 negatives in that time, all of which were processed safely. The last missions were flown on 26 November, when Kennedy personally began negotiations with Soviet Premier Nikita Khrushchev. The United Nations secretary-general, U Thant of Burma, offered to act as liaison between the two nuclear powers, but U.N. action was unnecessary and ineffective. In the end, the Russians backed down and withdrew their missiles. American naval supremacy, as expressed by a blockade of Cuba, and the yawning brink of nuclear war dictated a retreat. But this lesson of seapower was not lost upon the Soviets.

Other Crusader squadrons were involved in the Cuban crisis, but largely in passive roles. The *Essex* and *Independence* cruised the Caribbean, launching aircraft on searches and blockade patrol, but no shooting occurred. One of VFP-62's embarked detachments was aboard the *Enterprise*, but the bulk of surveillance was conducted from Key West.

After things settled down, President Kennedy paid a visit to "Fightin' Photo," and presented the squadron with a Navy Unit Commendation—the first ever awarded in peacetime. The ten photo pilots who flew Crusaders over Cuba all received at least one Distinguished Flying Cross, while the six navy fliers were awarded an aggregate of sixteen DFCs.

In January 1963 the president wrote Com-

37

mander Ecker personally, saying in part, "I would like to take this opportunity to reaffirm my thanks for your hard work during those weeks. As I said at our meeting in Boca Chica, the reconnaissance flights which enabled us to determine with precision the offensive build-up in Cuba contributed directly to the security of the United States in the most important and significant way."[11]

Crusaders continued experiments and testing in new roles even after they had been fully absorbed into fleet operations. In June 1963 an awesome, eerie feat was accomplished when the *Midway* was steaming off the California coast. An F-8D (previously F8U-2N) and F-4A made successive landings on the 13th. Nothing unusual—except that neither pilot touched his controls.

Lieutenant Commanders R. S. Chew, Jr., and R. K. Billings, both of NATC at Pax River, literally rode their planes down to hands-off carrier landings. Though experimentation toward this end had been under way since 1957, and research four years prior to that, these were the first fully automatic carrier landings made with production equipment. Guided from the ship, Chew's Crusader and Billings's Phantom both executed safe traps. The auto-landing system was nonstandard in Crusaders, but the *Midway* experiment showed the path to the future.

With all the operational developments, the clamor and the glamor of records and headlines, it was easy to overlook the day-to-day elements in the Crusader's success formula. Not the least of these was maintenance. A case in point was VF-124, the F-8 training squadron at NAS Miramar near San Diego. "We at the seat shop were very proud of our ejection-seat maintenance record on the F-8," recalled Roger Wenschlag, an aviation structural mechanic specializing in safety equipment.[12] During the period 1961–

1967, the Gunfighters recorded eighteen ejections, and seventeen pilots survived. Faithful to the Crusader, Wenschlag noted that few ejections were directly attributable to the aircraft itself. Frequently the undergraduate fighter pilots had to abandon their Crusaders after running low on fuel or overstressing the airframe.

Another aspect of F-8 maintenance was the "Buick hood." The F-8A and F-8C had an equipment compartment atop the fuselage, just forward of the wing. To gain access to the compartment, mechanics had to open the hatch, which was hinged at the rear. It reminded several mechs of a bit of their youth; the cover was named for the remarkable similarity to the 1941 to 1951 Buicks.

There were other elements of humor to F-8 operations, some more overt than others. There was the time at Miramar that a MiG killer, a colorful member of the Crusader community, pulled up to the fuel pit to top off his tanks. He waited several minutes and, receiving no service, taxied from the pits over to the line shack. Still the service crew failed to notice the waiting F-8. At this juncture, the pilot ran out of patience. With his portside next to the building, he extended his fuel probe through the window. Service was immediately forthcoming.

And then there was the *Hancock* squadron commander who noted the crew mustering to morning quarters in port at Yokosuka, Japan. Flying out of the "Bingo" field, NAS Atsugi, the CO descended to about 60 feet over the harbor, rolled 180 degrees, and made a beautiful inverted pass at flight-deck level. Just the way to start the day.

In the early 1960s, F-8 pilots began building ever-higher flight times in their Voughts. The first F8U pilot with 1,000 hours in type was Commander James B. Stockdale, who flew with VF-

211 and VF-24 from 1957 to 1960. In April of 1964, Lieutenant Commander B. C. Morehouse became the first of some sixty-five aviators to log 2,000 hours in Crusaders. The first marine to pass the 2,000 mark in F-8s was Lieutenant Colonel M. H. Sautter of VMF-232, at the end of his squadron's Vietnam deployment in August of 1967.

That was the year in which the F-8 observed its tenth anniversary in fleet service. By that time, Crusaders had logged over 1,500,000 hours of flight time and a quarter-million carrier landings. In 1968 the Joseph C. Clifton Trophy was awarded for the first time, an annual presentation to the outstanding fighter squadron in the navy. The initial recipient was VF-51, which had flown F-8s since 1960 and already had four Vietnam tours to its credit.

The Crusader probably flew more hours annually than any other navy fighter from 1960 through 1966. The big jump came in 1960, with 136,800 hours—a huge increase over the previous year's 87,500. When Phantoms finally outflew F-8s in 1967, it was by a margin of 188,500 to 173,000. From then on, the annual Crusader flight time diminished steadily to 1970, the last year in which F-8s logged 100,000 hours.

The Crusader's peak year was 1964, with 230,570 hours. The increased tempo of the following year was reflected in the F-8's career high of 47,885 hours of carrier flying.

Through it all, the Crusader worked under the burden of a high accident rate. In comparison with the Phantom, the F-8 was two or three times more likely to suffer a major accident. Taking 1969 as a representative year (the F-4's highest annual flight time), fifty-four Phantoms were involved in major accidents during the total 223,594 hours that navy and marine pilots flew them. Curiously, the same number of F-4s were destroyed or badly damaged in accidents during the preceding and following years. The 1969 figures, therefore, averaged a major Phantom accident every 4,140 flying hours. Twenty-one of those incidents occurred during the 44,343 hours of carrier flying, or one accident every 2,111 embarked flight hours. In 1969 Crusaders logged 112,516 hours with seventy-one major accidents—one every 1,584 hours. At sea F-8s flew 25,759 hours (roughly a quarter of their total for the year) with thirty-eight "majors." This meant that embarked Crusaders flew a mere 678 hours between incidents. In other words, F-4s were two and a half times safer in all flight hours, and three times safer aboard the ship.

Nevertheless, 1969 was not the Crusader's worst year, not by a long way. In 1962 F-8s incurred a whopping 106 major accidents, with 97 in 1963. In round numbers, these figures meant 1,800 and 2,000 hours between accidents. These totals were not significantly different from the then-new Phantom's one "major" per 1,900 and 2,100 hours for the same years. But then the situation changed dramatically.

In general terms, from 1961 (the F-4's first full year of service) until 1976, Phantoms were demonstrably safer than Crusaders. In only two of those years did F-8s record fewer major accidents per hours flown: in 1961 and 1964. Beginning in 1962, when F-4s started operating off carriers, the Crusader was already well established and had half the Phantom's problems at sea. After that, 1964 was the only year in which Crusaders did better.

Taking the overall view, F-8 jocks can claim one category in which they matched or exceeded their F-4 counterparts. The Crusader's takeoff accident record was as good or better than the Phantom's, ashore and afloat. In the ten years from 1961 to 1970, F-8s recorded fewer major takeoff accidents in five of those years. Flying

41

from carriers, they did better during four years. Therefore, the Phantom's two engines were not always a guarantee of a safer launch.

Pilot error is the most common cause of aviation accidents, but materiel failure is often responsible. At least three Crusaders suffered aileron disconnect, but two of those aircraft were saved. In the first incident, a VF-162 pilot returning to the *Oriskany* during 1966 rolled into a left-hand bank over the ship. When he centered his controls, nothing happened. He applied full right aileron and still the craft rolled to port. Nearly inverted, the pilot punched out and was quickly rescued, but the airplane went into the Tonkin Gulf and no assessment was made. The next time it happened, the aviator in peril had sufficient presence of mind to let the evolution complete itself. He continued the process, timing it nicely to make a wing-down landing, which allowed the cause to be determined. From then on, control linkages were inspected for impending failure.

Nevertheless, in many other instances pilot error—not materiel failure—has led to near-accidents. In fact, several such incidents have been saved from disaster only by the design features of the F-8. A few have been so spectacular that individual examination is warranted.

Murphy's Law governs Crusader operations, just as for any other aircraft. A corollary to that law dictates that whenever something does go wrong, it will always happen at the most inconvenient moment. In naval aviation, this means attempting to fly with the wings folded—usually at night.

The first recorded instance occurred in 1949 when a Douglas Skyraider pilot took off from NAS Charlestown, Rhode Island, with his outboard wing panels locked upright for storage. As with all prop-driven carrier aircraft, the AD's ailerons were located on the folding portion of the wings, near the tips. Thus, if the negligent aviator had attempted a turn, his ailerons would have acted as rudders. While he could probably have made a straight-ahead landing, the pilot abandoned the Douglas at 250 feet and parachuted to safety.

Since then, at least a dozen similar instances have occurred. Significantly, they involved seven Crusaders. But because the F-8's ailerons are inboard of the wing hinge, the pilots retained control and all got down safely. The Crusader incidents occurred between 1960 and 1969 and, like the other aircrafts' misadventures, they shared a similar scenario. The most common environment for wing-folded flight was during a "hot" refueling at night. Standard procedure called for wings to be folded in the gas pits. The darkness and distraction of refueling resulted in the pilots overlooking the little matter of unfolding the wings before takeoff.

Only one of the F-8 incidents occurred in daylight, and that was the first time, at Capodichino Airport near Naples, Italy. On 2 August 1960, Lieutenant Jack Barnes of VF-11 took off without checking his wing-lock position. But he climbed to 5,000 feet, feeling out the bird, slowly gaining confidence. He dumped most of his fuel to reduce the Crusader to safe landing weight, then made a 175-knot approach. It was over 50 knots faster than normal low-weight landing speed, but necessary to compensate for the reduced wing area. Barnes plunked the F8U down with only slight damage to the wing and wing-fold mechanisms.

Vought's publicists were understandably pleased with the results of Barnes' unplanned flight to notoriety. The navy, however, possessed equally strong (if opposite) reactions. *Time* magazine picked up the story and concluded that the manufacturer's pride, while not necessarily misplaced, seemed to overshadow the circumstances that fostered the incident.

The next Crusader "wingless" flight occurred three and a half years later. On 31 March 1964, Lieutenant Commander Thomas J. Hudner took off from San Clemente, California, and routinely activated the variable-incidence selector to lower his wing after liftoff. But the seven-degree cant remained, and then Hudner discovered why.

Tom Hudner was no stranger to adversity. He had been the fourth and last F4U pilot to receive the Congressional Medal of Honor, for landing behind Communist lines near the Chosin Reservoir in December of 1950 in a vain attempt to rescue a downed squadronmate. In the dark night sky, he climbed his Crusader to 10,000 feet and began experimenting. Banking to port, he nosed down slightly to impose a half-G negative load on the airplane. Under this mild stress the port wingtip dropped into place and locked. Hudner repeated the sequence to starboard, again successfully. He then lowered the wing manually and landed. His skillful airmanship has been called "one of aviation's miracles."[13]

Two marines have also joined the wings-folded club. Both were members of VMF(AW)-235 operating out of Da Nang Air Base in Vietnam. A major in the squadron, taxiing out for a night strike in August 1966, folded his wingtips to maneuver around a parked plane. He then took off without extending the wings, loaded with a half-ton of bombs and six Zuni rockets. Once aware of his unenviable predicament, the marine jettisoned his ordnance offshore and turned gently for home. He descended toward the mobile arresting gear at the end of the runway, and engaged the wires. But it was just one of those days for the hapless major. In addition to taking off with his wings folded, he also neglected to lower his landing gear.

Another 235 pilot should have stayed in bed one night nearly ten months later. But this flier had better luck than the major. The F-8E packed two tons of bombs besides six Zunis, and they were dumped before the Crusader warily banked around for Da Nang. The marine recovered at base, making 160-plus knots on final.

At NAS Miramar in 1966 and 1967, two navy pilots became numbers five and six in the Crusader "pit parade." The aircraft were F-8Es from VF-191 and VF-53, both of which departed the fuel pit at night without unfolding their wings, but both landed safely.

Number seven came in January of 1969. This incident differed from the others in that the pilot did not actually leave the field. Departing the fueling area, he accelerated down the runway in afterburner. The Crusader had

Wings folded, an RF-8G awaits launch aboard USS Roosevelt *during a Caribbean cruise in 1969. (U.S. Navy)*

just rotated when a traffic controller in the tower informed the aviator of his situation. The pilot reacted quickly. He chopped power, dropped his tailhook, and snagged the wires at the far end of the runway.

However impressive these flights were, they couldn't quite compete with another legendary Crusader feat.

A fresh-caught aviator was making his second familiarization flight in an F-8H. Paced by an instructor pilot in another Crusader, the new sport made touch-and-go landings at his home field. However, as a crosswind picked up to 16 knots, the instructor told his student that an arrested landing was advisable. The active runway had arresting cables at both ends as well as long-field arresting gear at 6,000 and 7,000 feet from the approach end.

On his next landing the new F-8H pilot lowered his hook, touched down 500 feet short of the first arresting gear, and rolled through the cables. But the hook skipped over the wires, and the Crusader added power, lifted off, and went around again. The second attempt resulted in another bolter, and the Hotel lifted off once more. But witnesses thought the new pilot over-rotated, as the F-8 was fish-tailing, nose-high, and settling.

Seconds later the pilot radioed, "I got something, this thing's not flying."[14] Immediately he selected afterburner, apparently in an attempt to maintain flying speed, but one second later he ejected at about 20 feet above the runway.

Now on its own, the pilotless Hotel proceeded another 600 feet straight ahead, touched down on its main gear, and snagged the arresting cables. It stopped near the left side of the runway, with moderate damage. Meanwhile, the pilot had parachuted into a lake alongside the runway.

This incident was too bizarre to escape the

attention of "Grampaw Pettibone," the bearded, cantankerous old sage of *Naval Aviation News*. A mythical figure of the monthly publication, Grampaw Pettibone passes judgment on unusual foul-ups in his column. His feisty, crochety comments serve to point out contributing factors in aircraft accidents, and how they might have been prevented. His verdict on this remarkable case: "Sufferin' catfish! This one takes the cake! I frankly must admit that this aircraft did a heck of a lot better without the pilot."[15]

An airplane that flies with its wings folded and lands itself without a pilot. Who could ask for more?

Speedster

3

The Crusader was a record-setter from the day of its first flight. And in the months following John Konrad's Mach-1 maiden flight in the prototype, the navy came to see that it had a thoroughbred in its stable. Therefore, it was small surprise when BuAer's sporting blood began to stir, and the navy set its sights on the world speed record for production aircraft.

North American's F-100 Super Saber held the record at that time, and navy plans were laid for an attempt at USMC Air Station Mojave, California, north of Edwards Air Force Base. Such endeavors are seldom kept secret for long, however. Serious (if friendly) rivalries began to emerge. North American had submitted a design in the navy fighter competition that was won by Vought, and now the industrious folks from Dallas wanted to unseat the Super Saber. But quite aside from the manufacturers' one-upsmanship was a political rivalry on a grander scale. In 1955 the Department of Defense was only eight years old. The navy had called a truce with its time-honored army adversaries, and then began waging war on a second front—against the air force.

The navy–air force feud revolved around

Commander R. W. "Duke" Windsor in the "Project One Grand" F8U-1 which in 1956 became the first production aircraft officially to exceed 1,000 miles per hour in level flight. (Vought)

49

Leader of the first Pacific-to-Atlantic crossing with shipboard launch and recovery was Captain Robert G. Dosé. He and Lieutenant Commander Paul Miller crossed the country in 3 hours, 28 minutes on 6 June 1957. (Dosé)

the aircraft carrier controversy. Were flattops really the floating dinosaurs the flying generals claimed, or was it the B-36s of the Strategic Air Command that comprised the overrated part of America's nuclear deterrent? The air force stated, correctly, that bombers were vastly cheaper and less vulnerable than ships. The navy countered, equally correctly, that land-based air lacked the range and response capability of carrier airpower, especially in Korean-type brushfire wars.

The controversy peaked in 1949 when a reduction in navy appropriations resulted in the "revolt of the admirals." Though the Korean War did much to bolster carrier construction, the navy–air force rift remained. As a result, anything that resembled competition between the two services was attended with all the fervor previously reserved for the army-navy football game.

The pilot chosen for the record attempt was Duke Windsor. He was thoroughly familiar with the F8U, having conducted the carrier qualifications, and had delivered several of the first production birds. But his prime credentials were found in his logbook. Aside from lengthy test-flight experience, he had more Crusader flight time than anyone else at Pax River, and therefore knew the F8U better than other military pilots.

Speed records came and went with regularity, but the Mojave endeavor was different. It was expected to make the F8U the first production aircraft to exceed 1,000 mph (870 knots) in level flight. Accordingly, it was called Project One Grand. Early tests indicated Windsor would have no problem pushing a "dash one" over the thousand mark, as he had been clocked at some 1,100 mph in unofficial tests.

But the political atmosphere imposed a

delay. The air force was preparing the newest Super Saber, an F-100C, for a similar attempt. And on 20 August 1955 the first C model, piloted by Colonel Horace A. Hanes, tripped the Edwards clocks at 822.135 mph. It was a headline-making feat for North American and the air force. Never before had an official world speed record for production aircraft been achieved in excess of Mach 1. The Super Saber's 1.25 represented a significant advancement in aviation.

A year later, things had settled down enough for the navy to take its turn. At the time the absolute world speed record was 1,132 mph (about 980 knots), held by Britain. After eight attempts, a delta-wing Fairey design had gained the record. But the U.S. Navy did not want to take the unlimited title. The reason was tactical, not technical; the Crusader could certainly do the job, but there was no need to disclose the new fighter's capability to the world—or, more accurately, to potential enemies. Duke Windsor was told to keep a tight rein on his mount and win the race by little more than a length. If he were clocked at anything over 1,000 mph, BuAer would be happy.

J. W. Ludwig of Chance Vought's development section organized the company project with seventeen people. By late August 1956, preparations were completed at the Naval Ordnance Test Station near China Lake, California. The National Aeronautics Association, responsible for documenting official record attempts for the world body *Fédération Aéronautique Internationale* in France, had installed a sophisticated array of cameras and timing devices. These included two radar-controlled cameras with 10-inch telephoto lenses that would show elapsed time on film. Eight smaller cameras were installed along the 15-kilometer (9.3-mile) course.

51

And as a final resort, an NAA official rested on his back, stopwatch in hand, to observe the Crusader's passage over the start and finish lines.

The cameras allowed a departure from previous procedure. Up to this point, high-altitude attempts had been flown only on days when contrails allowed visual tracking by cameramen. But the radar-guided Bowen cameras required no such assistance. Succeed or fail, the F8U's attempt would be fully covered from the ground and air, because three other jets with NAA officials aboard would monitor Windsor's progress.

FAI regulations called for two passes over the measured course. The official speed recorded was therefore an average of both runs. And since most of the estimated half-hour flight would be made in afterburner, Vought wanted every bit of fuel that could be crammed into the Crusader. Therefore JP-5 was pumped into the tanks through coils in a bath of dry ice—"a setup resembling an old-time bootlegger's still," remarked one Vought employee.[1]

Windsor already knew the course intimately, as he'd made eight practice flights around the Sierra Nevadas. This ensured that he had his reference points in mind, thereby remaining within the specified boundaries. His aircraft was the twelfth production F8U-1, loaded to standard operating weight, including four 20-mm cannon and the equivalent of a full ammunition load. The attempt was set for Tuesday, 21 August 1956.

Duke Windsor took off at 0650 from MCAS Mojave, 70 miles from China Lake, and climbed to 40,000 feet, where the two record runs would be made. It was a cloudless day, with perfect tracking conditions. Windsor went supersonic at 32,000 feet en route to his designated altitude. In all, he would cover some 400 miles during the flight, including supersonic turns to reposition himself over the course.

FAI rules were tight on this point. The pilot was allowed to descend no more than 328 feet or climb no more than 1,640 feet from his entry altitude. Therefore, Windsor had to watch his Mach 1 turns carefully, being coached by a radar controller to remain "inbounds." He flew a curved course to follow the earth's curvature for a constant altitude above ground level, which experts said added 67 feet to his flight profile.

Thus, the record attempt involved considerably more than merely shoving the throttle through the detent into afterburner. It called for precision flying, and for all the miles covered, the actual distance that mattered amounted to less than 20 miles on the ground.

The temperature was too high for contrails at 35,000 to 40,000 feet, but the radar-controlled cameras performed well and captured Windsor's flight. Thirty-two minutes after takeoff he was back on the ground, owner of the new national and world speed record for production aircraft. The three pace planes never acquired the Crusader to check its progress, and small wonder. Windsor's two runs averaged 1,015.428 mph— only 117 mph short of the absolute record held by the British, and 193 mph faster than the F-100.[2]

In 1957 Windsor flew his Crusader to the national air show in Oklahoma City, where Project One Grand was given the final touch. In establishing a new U.S. speed record, the Vought-navy team had won the prestigious Thompson Trophy. Admiral Arleigh A. Burke, chief of naval operations, was with Windsor to receive the award, and with good reason. In the twenty-seven-year history of the Thompson, neither Vought nor the navy had ever contested the event. Originally it was a closed-course pylon race, and the navy had little interest in such things. But following World War II, the Thompson had evolved into a contest for the country's straight-line speed record. For 1956, it went to the Crusader.

But 1957 was also a year of records and awards for the F8U. In June and July two transcontinental flights demonstrated the Crusader's exceptional potential through sustained high-speed cruising and in-flight refueling.

In late May, VX-3 at Atlantic City, New Jersey, was informed by OpNav in the Pentagon that President Eisenhower would be aboard the new carrier *Saratoga* in the Atlantic during the first week of June. Despite his army background, Eisenhower was good to the navy; almost one carrier a year was authorized or laid down during his administration. The navy wished to show its appreciation in suitable fashion, and turned to Captain Bob Dosé and VX-3.

The stage was set for a spectacular record attempt. Two Crusaders were authorized to make a west-to-east dash in the first ocean-to-ocean transcontinental flight by carrier aircraft. It was an imaginative idea, certain to gain attention. Feet-wet from the Pacific, feet-dry all across the continent, to a feet-wet landing in the Atlantic.

Dosé and VX-3 were well acquainted with the Crusader by now. There were plenty of experienced pilots to choose from, and Dosé selected Lieutenant Commander Paul Miller, his operations officer, to accompany him. A project officer on the F8U program and former Pax River test pilot, Miller was a good choice. The two flew to Dallas where Vought installed refueling probes in their early F8U-1s, then proceeded to the West Coast. They went aboard the *Bon Homme Richard* a week after leaving home, and were ready for the effort on 6 June.

The planning was complete. Bob Dosé and

Paul Miller launched from the "Bonny Dick" off the California coast and shaped course for Dallas. Eleven minutes out, they dove from 45,000 to 25,000 feet and rendezvoused with two AJ-2 tankers out of Carswell Air Force Base near Fort Worth. They plugged in to the Savages, topped off, and disengaged. The two Crusaders then lit the burners, rocketed back to 45,000 feet, and settled down to a .96 Mach cruise to Alabama.

Seventeen minutes short of the East Coast, the pilots chopped their throttles and Dosé led Miller into a steady descent. *Saratoga* was 50 miles off Jacksonville, Florida, and VX-3's landing signal officer, Lieutenant Commander Ken Sharp, was aboard. Determined to give the commander in chief a thrill, Dosé and Miller howled past the ship at bridge level, about 75 feet from the island, doing 600 knots indicated in line astern. The Crusaders honked abruptly into mind-blurring 7-G turns, doing 400 knots on the crosswind leg, and Dosé wondered, "Will we ever slow down?" It was uncertain, as he had 300 knots on the dial turning downwind and 250 on base.

Turning final, where Ken Sharp picked them up, Dosé and Miller still had 220 knots in hand—over 100 knots more than they needed. But by now the Crusaders were "dirtied up," with wheels and hooks down, flaps down, and wings elevated. At 140 knots Dosé continued his approach—still a bit fast—and plunked down on "Sara's" deck three hours and twenty-eight minutes after departing the *Bon Homme Richard*. Miller was right behind. The VX-3 team had established an unofficial transcontinental speed record. But not even the interview with Ike made as lasting impression on Dosé as one salient fact. Neither pilot had touched his throttle from 45,000 feet down to the deck—ample proof of how well they now knew the Crusader.[3]

Six weeks later the F8U set another transcontinental record, but this one was official. Like the VX-3 flight, the July effort was west to east, planned and executed in minimal time. However, this time the Crusaders were feet-dry all the way.

Project Bullet was run under the direction of Rear Admiral T. B. Clark, head of Naval Air Test Center, Patuxent River. But in large part it was instigated by Major John H. Glenn, Jr. Glenn, a 36-year-old marine fighter pilot, had flown F4Us in the Central Pacific and China during and after World War II. In Korea he was an exchange pilot with the air force, flying F-86s into MiG Alley, where he caused something of a sensation. In a mere eleven days the freckle-faced Ohioan claimed three Soviet-built MiG-15s, an accomplishment exceeded by only one other marine during the entire war.

After Korea, Glenn went to Pax River. He had been in flight test barely three years when Project Bullet arose. Basically, it hoped to fulfill a plausible but unrealized ambition: to accomplish a supersonic crossing of the United States. There was little doubt that the Crusader could do it, but until Glenn sold his boss on the idea, nobody had given it much thought. In this respect it was similar to Dosé and Miller's feat—an obvious record waiting to be set.

Admiral Clark stated the official purpose of Project Bullet was "to test the sustained capacity of the Crusader at near maximum power over a long distance."[4] A cross-country dash at Mach 1 would certainly do that. But it would also give the navy another chance to take the air force down a peg. The transcontinental record was then held by a Republic F-84F, which made the trip in three hours, forty-five minutes during March 1955. Dosé and Miller had already beaten that time by about seventeen minutes, but their record wasn't officially monitored and therefore didn't go into the books.

Bullet was approved in early July, with only

Major John Glenn, the future astronaut, who established a transcontinental speed record in an F8U-1P on 16 July 1957. (Peter B. Mersky)

two weeks to accomplish the mission. It made for a frantic schedule. As with Duke Windsor's closed-course record, NAA recognition had to be gained, logistics coordinated, timers arranged, and confirmation officially approved. A west-to-east crossing afforded the best prospects owing to the jet stream, so Los Angeles International Airport was designated the departure point. Floyd Bennett Field, New York, was the destination, some 2,446 miles from the point of launch.

Certain criteria had to be fulfilled ahead of time. In addition to NAA monitoring of the flight, alternate airports had to be designated. Weather patterns indicated possible—even probable—trouble around Los Angeles. And any last-minute changes in takeoff or landing site had to be within 60 kilometers (38 miles) of the geodetic center of the original fields. So NAS

Los Alamitos was chosen as the backup departure point.

While the navy and NAA were busy with their respective preparations, so were the pilots and Chance Vought. Glenn's wingman was Lieutenant Commander Charles Demmler. The two fliers went to Dallas to consult with Vought project engineer Augie Shellhammer. Among other things, they decided to use JP-5 fuel. Being heavier than standard JP-4, it would provide longer range in afterburner. Shellhammer and the two aviators estimated that each of the three in-flight refuelings would take eight minutes at most, and this procedure was part of Project Bullet's training. Considering the limited time available, the planning and rehearsal phase was unusually thorough. Demmler conducted numerous practice flights, experimenting with weather reconnaissance and tanker rendezvous, and his tests bore out the paperwork. Refueling tests were conducted at Dallas and Mojave with AJ-1 Savages from VAH-6, VAH-11, and from Pax River's flight-test department. The tankers then deployed to Albuquerque, New Mexico; NAS Olathe, Kansas; and NAS Columbus, Ohio.

Meanwhile, the two Crusaders were made ready. Glenn's aircraft received especially close scrutiny, as BuAer Number 144608 was only the third production F8U-1P. Demmler would fly a standard fighter, but Glenn was to photograph the country from coast to coast, and VFP-61 at NAS Miramar near San Diego prepared the cameras while other preparations went ahead.

By 15 July everything looked ready. At least, everything but the weather. Los Angeles meteorologists were so gloomy that support equipment and personnel moved to Los Alamitos in anticipation of a change in departure point. But the forecast for the scheduled mission date, the sixteenth, was much improved. Glenn and Demmler were to take off at 0600.

Actually, they launched four minutes late. To prevent further delay, the fuel tanks were topped off with engines running—the first time this procedure had been used. Then, at 0604, Glenn's photo bird, followed by Demmler's fighter, accelerated down the runway and was airborne.

An hour previously an A3D had departed Los Angeles to scout the weather for the F8Us. Glenn and Demmler climbed on top of the overcast at 35,000 feet and set course for Albuquerque, 700 miles east. Guided by radar vectors from Continental Air Defense Command, they came out of afterburner and descended to 25,000 feet to rendezvous with a Savage of VAH-11. Demmler was first to link up, but in the process his fuel probe was damaged. There was no choice but for Glenn to refuel and continue alone.

John Glenn's "Project Bullet" F8U-1P, BuAer Number 144608, was rebuilt as an RF-8G and assigned to VFP-63. The record-setting Crusader was lost in a landing attempt aboard Oriskany *(CVA 34) on 13 December 1972. The pilot safely ejected, however, into the Tonkin Gulf and was rescued. (Peter B. Mersky)*

The process was repeated over western Nebraska and Glenn's native Ohio. Along the way he had activated his cameras, obtaining a mosaic of the United States from coast to coast and horizon to horizon. After leaving the final tanker rendezvous, it was a short 530 miles to Floyd Bennett Field. Glenn made a slow decent over New York, and when he touched down at the naval air station, the clock stopped at 3 hours, 23 minutes. It was five minutes faster than Dosé and Miller's flight, averaging 725.55 mph, or slightly in excess of Mach 1 at average altitude. And Bullet was 21 minutes faster than the official F-84 record set two years before.

Glenn's record probably still stands as the fastest coast-to-coast crossing by a single-engine aircraft. But a better basis of comparison is an earlier feat. Thirty-five years before, in September of 1922, an army air corps pilot named Jimmy Doolittle flew a DH-4 biplane from Pablo Beach, Florida, to San Diego with one gas stop. His elapsed time: 22 hours, 35 minutes. It was the first time anyone had crossed the country in less than one day. But the Crusader put John Glenn in New York just fashionably late for lunch.

Four and one-half years later, of course, Glenn would set a more spectacular record. On 20 February 1962 he became the first American—and the only marine—to orbit the earth. Sadly, his F8U-1P did not fare as well. BuAer 144608 was remanufactured as an RF-8G and went to war aboard the USS *Oriskany* in 1972. Operating off the North Vietnamese coast, the photo bird was lost in a bad landing.

In part, Project Bullet was responsible for two other prestigious aviation awards that the F8U won for Vought and the navy. The Collier Trophy was presented "for concept, design and development of the first carrier-based fighter capable of speeds exceeding 1,000 mph."[5] It was only the second time a fighter had won the Collier. Then in 1958 the Bureau of Aeronautics awarded its Certificate of Merit to the Crusader, the first such award ever presented.

Impressive as the records were, gratifying as the publicity may have been, neither trophies nor headlines were the Crusader's intended goals. The F8U was meant to fight a modern air war, to engage and defeat enemy fighters and thereby secure air superiority. By 1964 it seemed as if the last Vought fighter would join the long list of good-to-excellent designs that providentially were never required to prove their worth in combat. But, for better or for worse, the Crusader was granted that opportunity beginning in its eighth year of fleet service. For events began drawing the United States into a part of the world that many people still called French Indochina.

F-8 Armament

4

The Crusader has employed a wide variety of ordnance and internal or external mission stores. But if Crusader pilots had a common dream during the Vietnam War, it was built around their guns. Recalled one F-8J pilot, "Every F-8 jock I knew had one big ambition. We all wanted to bag five MiGs with our 20-millimeters, never firing a missile, then go back to Miramar and lord it over the F-4 drivers."[1] Indeed, the Crusader's four Colt Mark 12 cannon accounted for much of the F-8 mystique. They also accounted for many of its problems. Both factors were apparent early in the new fighter's career.

One of the first units to experience difficulty was VX-3, during operational tests at Atlantic City in 1957. Captain Bob Dosé, the squadron commander, was well versed in aviation ordnance, and found the F8U-1's guns troublesome from the start. He recalls that the four 20-mm guns gave a 12-foot pattern at 1,000 feet in several early Crusaders, and a 12-mil dispersion was not conducive to superior marksmanship. By way of comparison, some Hellcat squadrons in World War II achieved a 3-mil pattern, for those pilots proficient enough in such precision gunnery.

Fleet squadrons also found problems with the F8U-1 guns. Fighting 103 reported excessive vibration from the gun mounts, sometimes causing dislocated instruments in the cockpit. The original fire-control radar also had flaws, and before the avionics were fixed, good pilots were achieving only seven or eight hits on a target sleeve from 200 rounds. In the Grumman Cougar or North American Fury at the same time, scores of 50 to 60 percent were not entirely unknown.

Less critical but bothersome problems also arose. The audio tone in the pilot's earphones, which normally told him his radar was tracking a target for a gunnery pass, frequently malfunctioned. And the ground safety switches, which blocked off the firing circuits when the landing gear was down, occasionally failed.

As the fleet gained more experience with Crusaders, the bugs were eventually worked out. Not everywhere, of course, but in those squadrons that worked at maintaining their guns, the 20-millimeters performed admirably. It merely took time. So when the Vietnam War rolled around, many F-8 squadrons were proficient at aerial gunnery. As the only "gunfighter" in the navy inventory, the Crusader was considered a pure air-superiority aircraft by its pilots and maintenance personnel. This attitude—which was actually a well-developed esprit—had much to do with the F-8's outstanding success in air combat.

Originally armed with 125 to 144 rounds per gun, the Crusader experienced a reduction in the 20-mm priority during the war. The Mark 12s fired some 660 rounds per minute, providing roughly 13 seconds of sustained fire. But as the bombing campaign over North Vietnam grew increasingly sophisticated, additional equipment was added to tactical aircraft. Chief among the new gadgets was an ECM pack. Electronic countermeasures were mandatory for planes operating in an environment of radar-directed flak and missiles, but the F-8 had precious little space to spare. Consequently, something had to give.

Colonel Roger Peard was the F-8 design officer at the fighter branch of the Bureau of Weapons in 1965. An experienced marine aviator with ample flight time in both fighter and photo Crusaders, Peard saw the need for F-8 ECM. Unfortunately, the only internal space for the black boxes was in the nose. This meant that the ammunition capacity had to be reduced in order to make room for ECM equipment. It was not a popular concept.

Any reduction in a combat aircraft's offensive payload is met with disfavor. After all, the historic trend is to add ordnance, not reduce it. Peard's concept was fought all the way up to the CNO's office, but in the end his proposal was adopted. The standard ammo load was reduced to squeeze the ECM package into the nose, and Vietnam-bound Crusaders possessed at least minimal threat warning.

Other problems with the guns surfaced at about this time. Early in the war, Naval Air Systems Command received many complaints about the 20-mm guns' failure to fire off a whole load. Expended brass shell casings were internally retained in Crusaders, rather than being ejected. The reasoning was sound: ejected brass at high speed (up to and including Mach 1) could damage the skin or tail surfaces. So the expended cases were captured in the fuselage for removal after landing.

Nevertheless, spent cases often piled up in the front of the ammo bays, clogging internal ejection chutes, which in turn led to malfunc-

An F8U-2 is loaded with a new supply of 20-mm ammunition. Standard load was 144 rounds per gun. (Gill)

tions. Pax River finally devised a metal finger at the chute exit that deflected the brass to the rear of the bay, and that fixed the problem. But other headaches remained. Broken breech-block locks and bulkheads ruptured by escaping gun gas were among the problems that required remedy from time to time.

Another gun-related problem was never fully solved. High G forces frequently jammed ammo belts in their chutes, preventing proper feed to the breeches. Related to a high-G load were other failures, such as incapacitated pneumatics that charged the guns. Another trouble that arose late in the F-8's career was that under some circumstances involving heavy landing weights, F-8Js had to fire off their ammo load in order to land aboard ship safely. "J-Birds" were the heaviest of the series, with additional avionics and boundary layer control, and landing weight was critical.

Through it all, though, Crusader partisans stuck to their guns. One tactical problem they encountered, though, was insufficient duration of fire while F-8s provided Rescue CAP (Combat Air Patrol) for downed fliers. Strafing was an important aspect of ResCap, either to keep hostile troops away from the rescue site or to suppress antiaircraft fire. But a ten-second supply of ammunition was far too little to accomplish the job, even with a full division on station.

Roger Peard became aware of the situation through VF-124 at Miramar. Recalled Peard, "I was impressed on every contact I had with that squadron, with its fierce loyalty to the Crusader as an airplane and weapons system."[2] As the West Coast F-8 training squadron, VF-124 frequently had to deal with evolving operational problems, and this time was no exception. The "Gunfighters" installed cockpit switches allowing the pilot to select the two top guns or the two bottom guns—one on each side—or all four at once. This effectively doubled the duration of firepower at no practical loss to effectiveness. Few ground targets required the use of four 20-mms at any one time, so the fix made good sense tactically as well as technically.

Chance Vought, informed of the change, endorsed it. Other squadrons heard of it and also made the simple wiring alteration. The snag came at middle-level maintenance inspection, such as the Overhaul and Repair Facility at NAS North Island. O and R complained that the change was unauthorized in navy maintenance manuals and wanted the new switches removed. Colonel Peard, still at BuWeps, consulted with VF-124 and helped them submit a proposed Air Frame Change to Air Systems Command. It was accepted and published, and the combat squadrons got on with the war.

As originally conceived, the Crusader's primary armament was to be its rockets. Two-inch unguided Gimlet and Redstone rockets were to be carried in a pack mounted in the speed brake beneath the fuselage. Up to sixty could be carried as an overload package, or in place of the four cannon. Fortunately, this concept failed. In 1955 development problems arose, and neither the Redstone nor Gimlet was available. So the speed-brake rocket launcher was modified to accept thirty-two folding-fin 2.75-inch rockets until the 2-inchers became operational. Then the whole idea was abandoned in the F8U-2 series, with no one lamenting its passing.

A far better option was first considered in February 1955. The Sidewinder heat-seeking air-to-air missile was advocated in BuAer, with one to be mounted on a pylon beneath each wing, or four in the internal armament bay. The latter would have required shortening the missile by three inches and adapting folding fins. Both were possible, but the idea never caught on. In August of that year, external fuselage rails were approved, and it was not until much later that under-wing missile pylons were added.

Thus, the Sidewinder became the Crusader's primary weapon. The situation was well stated by Captain Bobby Lee, a MiG killer, well after the war: "The Sidewinder missile is the best air-to-air weapon in the world, and I know of no fighter pilot who would disagree. Guns, as good as they are, are used as a close-in weapon after a missile firing position has been exploited."[3]

Sidewinder was developed by the Naval Ordnance Test Station at China Lake, California, in the early 1950s. Officially the Air Intercept Missile, Mark Nine, (AIM-9), the Sidewinder was well named. Its warhead possessed an infrared homing device that sought out the heat source of the target aircraft's engine. The heat-seeking AIM-9 was therefore named after the Southwest's famed rattlesnake—also a heat seeker!

Produced by Philco and General Electric, some 60,000 AIM-9Bs had been delivered by 1965. The most widely used version was the D, which weighed 160 pounds at launch, propelled by a solid-fuel rocket motor. Nine feet long, with a 10-pound warhead, the 'winder was effective at zero angle-off from about 1,000 feet to something over two miles behind a MiG-sized target.

Sidewinders were first used in combat in 1958, when Nationalist Chinese F-86s clashed with mainland-based Communist Chinese MiG-17s over the Formosa Strait. In fact, it is thought that one AIM-9 that struck its target failed to detonate, and a Communist MiG driver brought home a valuable prize. (The Soviet Atoll is a heat-seeker that bears an uncanny similarity to the Sidewinder.) Despite the combat experience gained by the Chinese, tests in the U.S. produced vastly unrealistic expectations of the AIM-9. Pre-Vietnam exercises led to the belief that Side-winders, and other air-to-air missiles, could achieve as high as 70 percent hit reliability. The real world of air combat quickly disproved the peacetime estimates. Throughout the war, the successes of Sidewinder firings ranged from 9 to 20 percent. Through the early portion of the North Vietnam aerial campaign only one launch in eleven scored a hit.

The Crusader's primary weapon was the AIM-9 Sidewinder, here being loaded onto a Ticonderoga *F-8 in 1964.* (U.S. Navy)

The fault was not the Sidewinder's. It was the difficulty of recognizing a missile's firing envelope, and the inexperience of U.S. aircrews in air-combat maneuvering. On the missile range back home, drones trundled along at an obligingly steady heading and airspeed. MiGs were decidedly less accommodating, and the F-4, F-105, and even F-8 pilots frequently had trouble achieving and maintaining a favorable firing position long enough to shoot.

In some cases, pilots missed sure kills by firing only one missile, which malfunctioned or went wide. When shooting for blood, the proper technique is to always fire twice, whether the target be man or beast. This lesson was eventually relearned in Vietnam, but only after many early opportunities were lost. Theoretically, Sidewinders could be launched with some prospect of success at deflection angles up to 40 degrees. But this was an optimistic figure, and few kills were made at more than 20 degrees angle-off.

Added to these problems was the compounding difficulty of the missile's performance envelope. The envelope changes with altitude, airspeed, and G load, so a pilot almost has to be a mathematician in order to determine when he's positioned for a good shot. In response to this situation, a partial answer was found.

An audio signal was piped to the pilot's earphones from the missile while on its rail. A low growling sound indicated that the 'winder was tracking a heat source. A higher-pitched tone informed the pilot that the missile was locked on and ready to kill—a concept identical to the audio gun tone, already mentioned. So sensitive was the IR homer that it could be checked before launch by shining a flashlight on the AIM-9's heat-seeking head. If the pilot heard the growl in his ears he knew the missile was functional.

But jet exhaust wasn't the only target that a

69

'winder could track. In January of 1968 two pilots of VF-162, flying off the *Oriskany*, found locomotives on North Vietnamese railways. In the first case, Commander Charles A. L. Swanson got a lock-on and scored a direct hit on the engine, causing "a tremendous explosion."[4] Two days later, Lieutenant Commander John S. Hellman's 'winder hit a locomotive's boiler behind the stack.

Still, there was room for error in rapidly changing air combat. Pilots tended to "pickle off" one or two missiles the first time they heard a tone. The grumble in their headsets often meant merely that the Sidewinder was tracking—not that it was positioned to home on a target. Pilots were trained to favor tone over boresight, since the missile "knew" better than the pegged-range gunsight if it were in range, and eager aviators often fired unsuccessfully at the first indication of a tracking tone.

The boresight pattern was important to a successful launch, though. While on the rail the missile's head was gimbaled to restrict tracking to a narrow arc in front of the aircraft. After launch, the head was gimbaled over a much wider limit, allowing a better chance of homing on a turning target.

A variation on the gimbal arc was included in the Sidewinder Expanded Acquisition Mode—SEAM for short. Intended to improve target tracking, the SEAM box allowed the missile head to follow the APQ-83 radar side-to-side sweep within a wider gimbal arc. This permitted a target tone somewhat off boresight, with effective radar lock-on during a ground-controlled intercept. In a hassle, though, with target bearings and ranges constantly changing, things happened too fast, and the best solution was to get to the target's six o'clock.

But that wasn't always possible. Therefore, a radar-guided Sidewinder was developed that performed in similar fashion to the big, sophisticated AIM-7 Sparrow. The AIM-9C, according to one veteran F-8 pilot, "didn't get the publicity in the squadrons that it deserved."[5] Though the -9C was proven in head-on attacks against drones at the Pacific Missile Range, it unfortunately wasn't widely used in combat. For unexpected targets that presented little or no heat source, the Sidewinder Charlie could be fired strictly by reference to the gunsight pipper (caged to indicate radar boresight), when a light indicated radar lock-on.

Tracking, of course, was of considerable importance. The APQ-94 radar in the F-8E was a powerful set, with a 60-nautical-mile search and 40-mile lock-on capability against bomber-sized targets. Thus, some squadrons expanded their air-to-air potential by flying with mixed Sidewinder armament: three AIM-9Ds and one radar-guided C. However, it is not recorded that any MiG kills were achieved with radar Sidewinders—probably for lack of opportunity.

Originally, F8U-1s carried only two rails on the fuselage for AIM-9Bs. This left the wings uncluttered for maximum fighter performance. But in 1964, multiple ejector racks were added, for two reasons. It was thought that Sidewinder accuracy would improve with a smoother launch from the wing, and an increase in firepower was thus achieved at the same time. Eventually Y rails allowed four Sidewinders to be carried on the fuselage stations, leaving the wings for other ordnance. The Crusader finally became a fighter-bomber.

With the F8U-2NE (F-8E), underwing hard points were added to give the Crusader a strike capability. The maximum external load was 4,000 pounds, with a considerable variety of weapons. Five-inch Zuni air-ground rockets, Bullpup air-ground missiles, and a selection of "iron bombs" were all employed.

71

The F8U-2NE, redesignated F-8E, was the first Crusader with a substantial strike capability. This test aircraft is armed with Bullpup B air-to-surface missiles under the wings and Zuni rockets on fuselage rails. (Vought)

Ordnance loads were varied to meet specific mission requirements. For instance, as many as eight Zunis could be carried with Y pylons; they were a useful load for flak suppression. Two Mark 84 bombs, one ton each, or six Mark 82s could be carried on underwing stations for strike missions. But experience showed up a serious release problem. When dropping in salvo, bombs tended to collide with one another, spoiling accuracy and raising the possibility of premature detonation. Therefore, minimum interval requirements were adopted that gave each bomb time to clear the aircraft before its companions followed.

Bombing performance is rated according to the CEP, or circular error probability. The CEP is a circle within which half of one's bombs are expected to fall. With most gravity bombs, the qualification score was a CEP of 100 feet. So if a pilot dropped six Mark 84s, three had to land within 100 feet of the target in order to qualify. But if he put half his load within a 50-foot circle, a pilot was rated expert.

Similarly, a 50-foot CEP was required to qualify with Zuni rockets, while a 25-foot circle containing half the rockets was an expert score. In neither case with air-ground ordnance did F-8 pilots possess bomb sights, as such. They used their gunsight in pegged range, figuring the mil lead to compensate for wind. In this respect, "seaman's eye" was just as important to Crusader jocks as it had been for their Corsair predecessors thirty years before.

Some F-8 squadrons were extremely proficient in the air-ground role. One of the best was VF-211, which outscored the three attack squadrons of Air Wing 21 during bombing competition in 1966! Some pilots who flew both the F-4 and F-8 in combat considered the Crusader a more accurate bomber, though opinion is divided on this point. However, considering that the Phantom began life as a VA design and was modified to the fighter-bomber role, while the F-8 was conceived as a pure fighter, its performance is all the more impressive if the two types were even roughly similar in bombing efficiency.

Because of the hazardous nature of flying in North Vietnam airspace, bomb and rocket attacks had to be made rapidly. The usual procedure was to approach at low level, stay low as long as possible, then climb to attack altitude near the target. The longer an aircraft was visible over the horizon, the greater its peril from antiaircraft defenses. Pilots generally rolled into 30- or 40-degree dives from 10,000 or 11,000 feet, dropping at 4,000 and recovering at 3,000. Recalled one combat veteran, "Below three grand was death" from intense small-arms fire.[6]

It is ironic that Crusader pilots, who before the war had arrogantly sneered at fighter-bomber pilots, found themselves engaged in

73

dropping bombs in Vietnam. The F-8 community seldom took much joy in hauling iron under its wings, but it could find pride in the skillful way it did the job.

Though Crusaders have excelled in the use of guns, rockets, missiles, and bombs, they also do well with a completely different "armament." For if knowledge is a weapon, then cameras are also a form of ordnance. And the reconnaissance-fitted Crusaders have maintained a long monopoly on the U.S. carrier-based light photo market. The first F8U-1P was the thirty-second production "dash one." In all, the photo birds

An RF-8's forward-looking camera provides a pilot's perspective of final approach to USS Oriskany. *(U.S. Navy)*

numbered 144 among the first 735 Crusaders, but in many ways they were different aircraft than the fighters. The undersurface of the forward fuselage was flattened to accommodate five camera stations, which in turn required re-plumbing much of the interior. Additionally, the upper portion of the fuselage was area-ruled in compensation for the increased fuselage cross section.

The -1P's stabilator was smaller than that of fighter Crusaders because the reconnaissance planes didn't require the "bite" of VF aircraft for ACM. The PR pilot's main asset is speed, and his very mission militates against jinking or maneuvering while trying to obtain worthwhile pictures.

The initial F8U-1P first flew on 17 December 1957, the fifty-fourth anniversary of the Wright Brothers' flight at Kitty Hawk, North Carolina. The remaining photo aircraft were built through 1958 and 1959, with final deliveries in early 1960. Two years later they were redesignated RF-8As, though over the years seventy-three were rebuilt as G models. Added features included ventral fins, strengthened wings, new electronics and avionics, and modified camera bays.

Originally, the -1P carried three trimetrogon and two vertical cameras, a combination that allowed overhead, forward, and oblique coverage. In the Gulf, only four cameras were required to perform the same job. Station One close to the underside of the nose was a movie or still camera. Station Two provided a 180-degree panorama. Stations Three and Four (port and starboard) covered 15 to 86 degrees vertically with KS-87 cameras.

The RF-8G was not stressed to the same extent as the fighters, but didn't need to be. Design loads of plus 6.4 and minus 2.4 Gs were more than ample for the requirements imposed upon

75

photographic aircraft. But one aspect of the photo-recce design had an aerodynamic effect all its own. The flat belly tended to act as a lifting surface, which promoted floating on landing. It also may have improved the glide angle.

Before infrared photography became widely employed, photo Crusaders usually relied upon photo-flash bombs for nocturnal reconnaissance. Commander R. A. Koch of VFP-62 experimented with new techniques during 1962—the same year that this unit made headlines with its coverage of the Cuban missile crisis. Koch operated two aircraft, one at 2,000 and one at 3,000 feet above the target. A modified vertical camera was angled to shoot forward at 15 degrees depression in the higher aircraft, while the lower RF-8 dropped flares of 110 million candlepower. RA-5 Vigilantes also possessed this capability, but the Viggies were never as widely employed as Crusaders.

The premier light photo squadron to cover the Vietnam War was VFP-63 from NAS Mir-

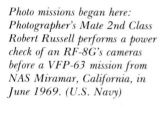

Photo missions began here: Photographer's Mate 2nd Class Robert Russell performs a power check of an RF-8G's cameras before a VFP-63 mission from NAS Miramar, California, in June 1969. (U.S. Navy)

amar. The squadron provided small detachments to WestPac carriers, and had personnel and aircraft almost constantly at sea during the entire war.

Most photo missions involved one RF-8 escorted by a fighter Crusader, usually following the recce plane at the four- or eight-o'clock position. Flying at 4,000 feet kept the carrier planes above small-arms fire, while allowing room to outmaneuver most SAMs. But it did not solve the heavy AAA threat.

"Unarmed and unafraid" is the typical recon-pilot's boast. With no more firepower than a .38-caliber revolver in a shoulder holster, the PR pilots penetrated the most sophisticated air defense network on the planet almost every day for eight years. Whether they were unafraid may be a matter of conjecture, but they never failed to get their pictures as long as their aircraft could still fly.

The Vietnam Years

5

The Crusader was the first U.S. Navy aircraft to get involved in the Vietnam War. In May 1964, the USS *Kitty Hawk* was cruising the South China Sea off South Vietnam. The political situation in the area was unstable at best, and recent leftist activity in Vietnam and Laos was judged of sufficient concern to warrant aerial surveillance.

Therefore, RF-8As were launched on photo-recon missions over Communist-controlled portions of Laos. Washington was interested in keeping track of any Pathet Lao activity that might threaten the neutral government of that country, and Crusaders were the best means available. Embarked recce aircraft included detachments of VMCJ-1 and VFP-63.

One of the most active PR pilots was Lieutenant Charles F. Klusmann. He flew a mission on 21 May, encountering stiff ground fire. It was not an unusual event, for guns up to 37 mm were available to the Laotian insurgents from Chinese or Russian sources. On this sortie, Klusmann's Crusader was hit and began to burn. He turned eastward, making for the *Kitty Hawk*, with the fire unabated. In fact, it burned for about twenty minutes before extinguishing itself, and Klusmann recovered without further incident.

Two weeks later, on 6 June, Klusmann's RF-8 was again hit by antiaircraft fire. But there was no getting home this time. He bailed out and parachuted safely to the ground, but he literally had jumped from the frying pan into the fire. Hostile troops began searching for him, and when a rescue helicopter from the *Kitty Hawk* approached, Klusmann signaled it to keep away. The chopper crew soon learned why. Communist soldiers opened fire, hitting the helo, which had no option but to return to the ship. Chuck Klusmann was captured and spent the next three weeks as a prisoner, but later managed to escape and make his way to safety.

Air Wing 11 continued its recon flights the next day. But in view of Klusmann's misfortune, a fighter accompanied each photo bird. Ironically, the same day armed recces began, 7 June, one of the F-8Ds was shot down. Commander Doyle Lynn of VF-111 ejected from his stricken Crusader and landed in the jungle, where he spent an uncomfortable night. Providentially, he was rescued, but the flights over Laos boded ill for the future. Conventional antiaircraft fire, whether from Laotian or North Vietnamese guns, had shown itself effective against low-flying jets.[1]

Meanwhile, the continuing need for fighters to escort RF-8s over Laos raised some questions at CinCPacFleet. The *Kitty Hawk* was soon to leave the line, and although the *Constellation* already was in position to take the duty, "Connie" had no F-8 fighters. Her VF squadrons flew F-4s, and at that time the deployed Phantoms had no air-to-ground capability. Therefore, they were useless as photo escorts.

But help was on the way. In April the *Essex*-class carrier *Ticonderoga* passed through Pearl Harbor, westbound. She operated two Crusader squadrons in Air Wing Five, including the Screaming Eagles of VF-51, who had demon-

79

strated air-ground competence in their Operational Readiness Inspection. In fact, Fighting 51 had developed its own strike capability during workups in the Chocolate Mountain region of Arizona. The squadron's F-8Es were equipped with newly fabricated Zuni rocket pylons and bomb racks in advance of formal approval.

On Sunday, 8 June, the "Tico" was at sea off Subic Bay in the Philippines when CinCPac ordered VF-51 to fly westward to the *Constellation*. The maintenance personnel were transferred to a destroyer at sea and delivered to Connie a day later. The *Constellation* then took over "Yankee Team" photo operations, with her embarked RF-8s and marine photo birds from Iwakuni, Japan. When the recon flights resumed on the tenth, VF-51 performed escort duty. The impromptu arrangement continued until 29 July when Connie headed for port and VF-51 returned to the *Ticonderoga*, the new Yankee Station carrier.

Tico arrived just in time. The Vietnam War was about to begin in earnest.

American destroyers steaming in international waters reported two attacks by North Vietnamese torpedo boats during the first week of August. In the initial encounter, the *Ticonderoga* had four F-8Es airborne and directed them to the aid of the destroyer *Maddox* the afternoon of the second. Commander Jim Stockdale, the first thousand-hour F-8 pilot and now leader of VF-51, directed his wingman and a section from VF-53 into attacks with 5-inch Zunis and 20-mm against three PT boats. In all, the Crusaders made six passes, firing eight Zunis and considerable cannon ammunition from low level. Stockdale's wingman, Lieutenant (j.g.) R. W. Hastings, sustained a hit in one wing and headed for Da Nang, where the skipper watched him land safely before returning to the Tico. The F-8s had left one torpedo boat burning, dead in the water, while the other pair made for the coast.

In response to the North Vietnamese attack, the destroyer *Turner Joy* was ordered to join the *Maddox* while the *Constellation* sortied from Hong Kong to reinforce the *Ticonderoga*. When the PT boats reportedly returned the night of the fourth, Jim Stockdale was again on hand. His wingman aborted with electrical failure, so the VF-51 skipper waged a lone "war" against phantom targets reported by the two destroyers. Taking vectors from the ships, Stockdale expended most of his ordnance—even a Sidewinder—at invisible bogies. It was a pitch-black night, and though the squadron commander saw the DDs' wakes and gun flashes, he glimpsed not so much as a trace of the alleged PT boats. To the man with the best seat in the house, the second Tonkin Gulf incident was a non-event.

Washington had other ideas. Early the following afternoon, the two carriers launched sixty-four aircraft for strikes against North Vietnamese naval and petroleum facilities. President Lyndon Johnson announced the retaliatory raids before the carriers had all their planes airborne, and then Secretary of Defense Robert S. McNamara named the targets while the planes were en route. Presumably the Vietnamese would have too little time to react.

But the carriers were 300 to 400 miles from their targets. According to one estimate, the North Vietnamese had roughly ninety minutes to prepare. In any event, they were not caught by surprise.[2]

Ticonderoga's Air Wing Five launched thirty-four planes, including sixteen F-8Es of VF-51 and VF-53. Six of the latter struck PT boats at Quang Khe, about 60 miles above the border, where eight boats were destroyed and twenty-one damaged by rocketing and strafing. Commander Jim Stockdale's Screaming Eagles, with

A-4s of VA-55 and -56, plus some A-ls, went after the two oil-storage dumps at Vinh. Not a bomb landed outside the cyclone-style fence surrounding the fuel depot, and as the planes pulled off the target, smoke from raging oil fires topped out at 14,000 feet. On the way home, VF-51 hit stray PT boats, flak sites, and suppressed antiaircraft fire with Zunis.

But it wasn't a one-sided battle. Forewarned, the AA gunners hit one Crusader that had to divert into Da Nang, South Vietnam. And two "Connie" pilots failed to return. A propeller-driven Skyraider went down with its pilot, and an A-4 driver bailed out to become a prisoner. It would not be the last time Robert McNamara's stupidity cost American lives.

So began the Vietnam War. Americans had died in Indochina before the summer of 1964, but they had been serving in advisory capacities. Now the United States commenced its slow but steady buildup of men and materiel, characterized by any number of Pentagonese catchwords. "Controlled escalation" and "graduated response" were in vogue for quite some time before anybody began to wonder just what they meant. Basically, the Johnson administration's policy enunciated in February of 1965 was that of tit for tat. There was no intention or willingness to apply sufficient force against North Vietnam to attempt a conclusion. Instead, air raids were made on an irregular basis until that spring, when the campaign became more or less permanent.

It was called "Rolling Thunder," and it was based upon a concept that bore little resemblance to the reality of the situation. McNamara's "whiz kids," the young civilian innovators in DOD, saw the world in a logical, orderly fashion. If X amount of pressure were applied to North Vietnam in gradually increasing intensity, the Communists would logically submit at point Y.

It was twentieth-century reasoning, quantified and computer-analyzed. And it amounted to a strategic error that would have been obvious to a Julius Caesar or a Genghis Khan. The tweedy decision makers in Washington consistently underestimated their enemy.

Rolling Thunder began in the southern portion of North Vietnam. The theory held that as the bombing line gradually moved north, nearer Hanoi, the Communists would lose their willpower and accede to a cessation of hostilities throughout Indochina. Therefore, from the beginning, the Vietnam War became a test of resolve as much as a clash of arms.

With increasing air operations, losses rose accordingly. On 11 February, over one hundred aircraft from three carriers struck Chan Hoa. Antiaircraft artillery (AAA) knocked down three planes: an A-1, an A-4, and a *Coral Sea* F-8D of VF-154. This time the pilots were rescued.

On 26 March, the *Coral Sea* and *Hancock* launched strikes against radar sites in North Vietnam and on tiny Bach Long Vi Island in the Tonkin Gulf. A Crusader and a Skyhawk were lost, but the two aviators survived.

New aspects of combat flying were inaugurated during this same period. On the night of 15 April, Air Wing 15 launched six A-4s and six Black Knights of VF-154 in company with Phantoms from the *Midway*. It was the first nocturnal armed reconnaissance mission of the war, and it proved uneventful. All aircraft returned to the *Coral Sea* and *Midway*.

For the aviators tasked to execute Washington's halfway measures, each at the risk of his one and only life, the war was seldom satisfactorily conducted. But the professionals' attitude was summed up in the popular saying, "It's the only war we've got." Nevertheless, that did not make some aspects easier to swallow. Tactical units operated under extremely tight control, not merely from task-force or area commanders, but from the Pentagon itself. The "rules of engagement" were closely defined and severely limiting. Squadron commanders at this stage of the war had little or no latitude in mission planning. For instance, no pre-strike reconnaissance was allowed, though the reason for this was ambiguous. Mission scheduling, even routes, were planned with little regard to weather—sometimes not even to terrain. Targets were limited, and alternates sometimes not even designated. Unexpended ordnance could not be dropped on targets of opportunity, but had to be jettisoned into the sea.

Frequently those targets that were on the "permitted" list seemed unprofitable, in view of the attendant risks. Aviators referred to the "Phu Ly bicycle repair facility," or the "Dong Ha oxcart inspection yard."[3] Furthermore, the type, number, and even the fuzing of bombs and rockets were usually specified by Washington. At one point, circa 1966, the State Department was calling the bomb loads. In short, the military command system was reduced to little more than a communications channel.

Enemy transport was vulnerable throughout the North, and trucks were among the early permitted targets—but only *military* trucks actually *traveling* on roads. How a fighter-bomber pilot attacking from 3,000 feet at over 500 knots was expected to identify a civilian vehicle was left to the imagination. Eventually a "lenient" policy was adopted that allowed trucks to be hit within 300 meters of roads. Other less ambiguous targets were barracks, radar stations, and ammunition dumps—as long as they were outside a sanctuary area and not near a civilian facility.[4] Since the entire population of North Vietnam was devoted to prosecuting the war, the value of this policy eluded most combatants.

While the air war over the North slowly increased in tempo, activity also increased in the South. As a matter of routine, carrier air wings broke into combat by flying strike and ground-support missions over South Vietnam before heading north to the Tonkin Gulf. But the navy had no monopoly on the F-8 war.

The RF-8As of VMCJ-1 were active from the spring of 1964. But marine Crusaders shot more than pictures. The F-8Es of VMF(AW)-212 under Lieutenant Colonel Charles H. Ludden flew with *Oriskany*'s Air Wing 16 from March to December of 1965. The Lancers had trained as fighters, but performed as bombers over North and South Vietnam. They were the only marine squadron so employed aboard Seventh Fleet carriers during the war.

The marines, with a 30-year-old patented technique of close air support, helped introduce tactical airpower to South Vietnam. And they made their presence felt. Marine and navy tac air so impressed the army theater commander,

The RF-8G's "armament" is shown in four camera positions, which allowed forward, lateral, or oblique photos. (U.S. Navy)

General William Westmoreland, that he requested semipermanent carrier assignments off South Vietnam. The policy was officially adopted in mid-May 1965 with the establishment of "Dixie Station," roughly 100 miles southeast of Cam Ranh Bay.

At the end of 1965 most marine squadrons were consolidated at Da Nang. The two carrier-based units, VMF(AW)-212 and detachments of VMCJ-1, were transferred from their ships and put on the beach. Phantoms and Skyhawks became the most numerous marine aircraft in-country, but the Crusaders were also well represented. The famed Checkerboard squadron, VMF-312, had arrived at Iwakuni, Japan, in June 1965 as part of Marine Air Group 13. Flying F-8s since 1959, the unit was now equipped with twenty-one Echoes and a complement of 24 officers and 171 enlisted men. Lieutenant Colonel Richard B. Newport took VMF-312 to Da Nang in mid-December, where operations began quickly. By the end of January 1966, 718 missions had been flown, at which time the Crusaders were transferred to VMF-235.

One VMF-235 pilot discovered that the in-country war was rather different from what he imagined. Captain Jack Patton, a reservist, had originally flown with VMF-321 and transitioned from FJ-4 Furies to Crusaders in 1965. He re-

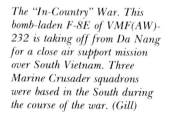
The "In-Country" War. This bomb-laden F-8E of VMF(AW)-232 is taking off from Da Nang for a close air support mission over South Vietnam. Three Marine Crusader squadrons were based in the South during the course of the war. (Gill)

called, "After learning the F-8's tremendous potential for air combat maneuvering, I determined to become the first marine ace of the Vietnam War, so I volunteered for a one-year tour of active duty."[5]

Eventually Patton joined the Death Angels, but he did little more than drop bombs. As the last F-8 squadron in South Vietnam, VMF-235 was engaged wholly in close air support, and Patton never got so much as a whiff of a MiG. Upon completion of his tour in 1968, he transferred to a reserve squadron and was in VMF-511 when they turned in their Crusaders in 1972. There were hundreds of Jack Pattons in Crusader cockpits during the war: well-trained, eager pilots, confident in the F-8, who never got a taste of air combat.

It should not be inferred, however, that all air ops over the South were milkruns. The tangible results were usually disappointing: bombs, napalm, or 20-mm fire directed at a treeline or map reference. Smoke from the forward air controller's marker rocket was frequently the only target. But the enemy had automatic weapons and occasionally shoulder-mounted Soviet heat-seeking missiles. Losses were low, even allowing for aircraft destroyed on the ground during rocket and mortar barrages, but only a fatalist or a crapshooter took the odds for granted.

That was exactly what the Red Devils of VMF-232 discovered. After spending four years in Hawaii with MAG-13, Lieutenant Colonel Nicholas M. Trapnell's squadron moved piece-meal to Da Nang via Iwakuni in late 1966. The Red Devils, one of the oldest marine squadrons, had received F-8Es in August, and the last elements arrived at Da Nang in December as part of MAG-11. They began operations before year's-end, dropping 418 tons of ordnance in I and II Corps, and in a limited area north of the DMZ. In the course of these early sorties, four

Illustrating the firepower concentrated in flak posts throughout North Vietnam is this antiaircraft battery, photographed in 1967. Five of the eight positions are occupied by 57-mm guns, with communications and radar control posts in the center of the site. Despite the vaunted surface-to-air missiles and MiG interceptors, gunfire accounted for 85 percent of all known U.S. aircraft losses over the North. (U.S. Air Force)

Crusaders were hit by ground fire, but all returned safely.

Over the next four months, from January to April 1967, 232's Echoes were hit nineteen times, most frequently by single small-arms rounds. But their luck didn't hold much longer. On 4 May, while circling a suspicious area, a Crusader took a hit and began trailing smoke and flames. The pilot headed east and decided it wasn't worth the risk to stick it out. He ejected, landed in the water, and was picked up unharmed.

Two weeks later, during a close-support mission, Captain H. J. Heilbach radioed that he was being fired upon. Apparently his controls were

damaged, for shortly after heading for the coast his F-8 pitched nose up, dropped straight down, and exploded on impact. Heilbach apparently made no effort to eject. In late June another pilot was lost when he punched out after reporting unspecified problems. Though he made a safe ejection, he did not survive.

Losses continued into July. Another F-8E fell to ground fire, but this time the aviator got out safely. But on the fifteenth, Viet Cong rockets ripped into Da Nang, and two Crusaders were destroyed where they sat. It was an eerie feature of the war in the South. Pilots might kill dozens of unseen Communist troops, or destroy ammunition stashes, and never know it. All they knew for sure was what happened when they were on the receiving end.

When 232's tour ended in August 1967, the Red Devils rounded out eight months of combat operations. They had flown 5,785 sorties for a total of 7,273 hours, dropping 6,271 tons of ordnance. Six Crusaders had been lost, and two pilots. That was Vietnam: numbers, statistics, estimates of damage inflicted, and known friendly losses.

Meanwhile, there was plenty else to occupy the thoughts of the carrier pilots and staffs. On 5 April 1965, a *Coral Sea* RF-8A photographed a surface-to-air missile (SAM) site 15 miles southeast of Hanoi. The new Task Force 77 commander, Rear Admiral Eddie C. Outlaw, initiated requests through channels to destroy the site before it became operational—a prudent enough precaution that was nonetheless denied. The rationale held that Russians undoubtedly manned the SAM battery, and Washington did not wish to offend the Soviets. For the same reason, Communist shipping in Haiphong harbor enjoyed immunity throughout the war.

Unimpeded, the Russians and North Viet-

An Oriskany *Crusader drops napalm in a treeline near Hue in November 1965. Carrier-based F-8 squadrons frequently engaged in close air support missions over South Vietnam—usually as a breaking-in period before moving "up north" to Yankee Station and more difficult jobs over North Vietnam.* (Naval Aviation News)

namese proceeded with their antiaircraft defenses. A second SAM site was found in July, and only after some air force planes had been shot down by the missiles were strikes authorized against them. Eventually F-8s would play a part in suppressing antiaircraft defenses, but that was yet in the future.

A new threat manifested itself about this same time. On 3 April, during a strike against bridges within 70 miles of Hanoi, the *Coral Sea* and *Hancock* planes were bounced by MiG-17s. The swept-wing fighters made one firing pass, inflicting no damage, and kept going. It had been eight months since intelligence reports indicated the arrival of MiGs in North Vietnam, but until now they had remained inactive. Presumably they used the intervening period for operational training. From now on, however,

An RF-8's overhead view of the Haiphong power plant following a strike in April 1967. (U.S. Navy)

they would remain a factor in all mission planning.

Since the inception of Rolling Thunder in February, air operations had spread over much of North Vietnam. By late fall, the bombing campaign was such that the country was divided into six regions called Route Packages. These "route packs" were numbered from south to north in order to designate operating areas for American aircraft. Route Packs I through IV extended from the border northwards about 250 miles. There, in the wide upper part of the country, RPs V and VI were divided by a north-south line about 30 miles west of Hanoi. Route Pack V therefore contained the northwestern part of North Vietnam, with several important lines of communication from China. And RP VI, the hottest spot, encompassed the northeast, with Hanoi, Haiphong, and the main coastal facilities.

Combined air force and navy strikes had so far done an effective job against North Vietnamese transport systems in permitted areas. By May of 1965, for instance, twenty-seven bridges had been attacked south of the twentieth parallel, and twenty-six had been destroyed.[6] The remaining span was the Thanh Hoa rail and highway bridge in Route Pack IV. A massive concrete-and-steel design of 540 feet across the Song Ma River, it was called the Dragon's Jaw by the Vietnamese. The Thanh Hoa Bridge was an important communication link to the south, and military supplies moved across it daily.

Since Hanoi was still out-of-bounds, the other major bridge in North Vietnam was safe. This was the Paul Doumer Bridge, just east of Hanoi. The "battle of the bridges" would form a central part of the air offensive over the North for the next several years, and Crusader participated in many of the attacks. In the twelve months following June 1965, carrier planes hit Thanh Hoa an average of twice a month, without

91

The Thanh Hoa Bridge, 65 miles south of Hanoi, was perhaps the toughest target in North Vietnam. At least 13 U.S. aircraft, including 2 RF-8s, were downed in attacks against the bridge before it was toppled in 1972. (U.S. Navy)

long-term effect. The fact was, the U.S. armed forces lacked the ordnance to knock out such a massive target. The Dragon's Jaw was rendered unserviceable for a few days at a time, but the 2,000- to 3,000-pound bombs necessary to destroy the structure were then unavailable.[7]

Furthermore, the bombing did not amount to anything resembling a consistent campaign, as in World War II or even Korea. Periodic halts were called by Washington, either for assessment or in hopes of favorable political response from Hanoi. In turn, the Communists used each respite to reinforce their defenses. From the end of 1965 to late February 1966, for instance, the ratio of missions encountering antiaircraft fire increased threefold.[8]

Other factors affected the tempo of aerial activity. At this stage of the war, the number of carriers "on the line" varied from two to four. They were frequently *Essex*-class ships, modified to the "27-Charlie" configuration with angled decks. Their air wings were largely composed of Crusaders and Skyhawks, as the larger *Midway* and *Forrestal* CVAs employed the heavier Phantoms and Intruders. Therefore, F-8s represented half or more of embarked fighters in the Tonkin Gulf for the first four or five years of the war.

The major effect upon air ops, however, was weather. When the southwest monsoon blew from late April to mid-October, the weather over North Vietnam was tolerable. The three months from June through August were best. During the rest of the year, when the monsoon shifted to the northeast, flying conditions were unpredictable at best. More often, they were wretched.

Thus, less than six months in twelve were conducive to flying by visual flight rules. In most circumstances, poor weather favors the defense, and certainly it was true in Indochina. Low clouds and heavy rain hampered visibility and frequently reduced it to almost nothing. This meant that targets were often obscured or fully hidden, and navigation was further complicated.

From a tactical viewpoint, poor weather made a tough job tougher. In order to visually identify landmarks, initial points, and targets, pilots were forced to fly below the cloud cover. Low ceilings therefore put aircraft well within range of automatic weapons, restricting the pilots' maneuvering room. SAMs were particularly hard to evade in low visibility, since the first rule in coping with them was, "You can't beat 'em if you can't see 'em." Not even flying in clouds or rain hid aircraft from most heavy-caliber guns or SAMs, since the batteries were inevitably radar-controlled.

American fliers over North Vietnam were therefore caught in an unenviable situation. They were required to play in their opponents' backyard, according to their rules. Under these circumstances, the object was more to survive than to win.

USS Hancock *(CVA 19) a WW II* Essex-*class carrier modified with an angled deck, steam catapults, enclosed bow, and other upgrades in the 1950s. "Hanna" and other Project 27C ships were exclusively deployed with F-8 fighter squadrons during the Vietnam War. (Peter B. Mersky)*

Survival frequently depended upon the capriciousness of fortune. One pilot who early on discovered the mixed blessings of surviving only to be captured was Commander Jim Stockdale. The first pilot to log 1,000 hours in Crusaders, he had led VF-51 in the initial retaliatory strikes against North Vietnamese PT boat bases in 1964. By the summer of 1965, Stockdale was skipper of the *Oriskany*'s Air Wing 16. Before deploying to Yankee Station, his F-3 squadron, VF-161, was replaced by VMF(AW)-212 with F-8Es to match the equipment of VF-162. Because the Demon lacked range and was incapable of supersonic level flight, VF-161 transitioned to Phantoms, but F-4s didn't operate from *Essex*-class carriers. So Air Wing 16 went to war with two Crusader outfits.

That suited Stockdale's taste. He alternately flew F-8s and A-4s as CAG, but he found the Crusader well suited to the job. He carried Zunis with phosphorous warheads to mark targets for his dive bombers, as the plumes of smoke provided a well-defined aiming point for fifteen minutes. This, combined with the F-8's accurate rocket delivery, was just what a strike leader needed. But Stockdale went further. Air Wing 16 made first combat use of 2,000-pound bombs on Crusaders. While the plane then required a catapult launch with reduced fuel for safe takeoff weight, the added strike potential was worthwhile. Once airborne, the Voughts topped off their fuel loads from waiting tankers.

In early September 1965, Stockdale was flying an A-4 while leading a strike against railway targets near Thanh Hoa. He'd bombed a train and begun his pullout when the Skyhawk was hit by 57-mm flak. Stockdale punched out just before his plane dived into the ground. Immediately seized, he was rolled down a street, kicked and beaten, then thrown into prison with a broken shoulder and leg. For seven and a half

The variety of naval aviation is shown in this 1966 photo as a VFP-63 RF-8G passes over A-1H Skyraiders of VA-52. The aircraft were off USS Ticonderoga *in Philippine waters.*

years he was the senior American in Hoa Lo prison, resisting threats and torture, keeping other POWs organized. Probably no one has lived to earn a Medal of Honor under more adversity.

Other pilots narrowly avoided similar fates. In April 1966, near the end of its second Vietnam deployment, *Ticonderoga*'s Air Wing 5 launched a fifteen-plane strike against a highway bridge near Haiphong. Eleven A-4s and four F-8Es, led by the respective squadron commanders, approached from behind a ridge north of the target. At least two SAMs were fired during the run-in, but the carrier pilots jinked in effective evasive action.

Then a 37-mm battery opened fire, and the two lead aircraft were both hit. Commander Stockdale's former shipmate, Commander Robair Mohrhardt of VF-53, found himself with

95

Refueling over the Tonkin Gulf, a Ticonderoga *Crusader plugs into a Douglas KA-3B tanker in 1966. (Harrison)*

an in-flight fire. But at this point there was no choice but to continue. Another pair of SAMs flashed by, and then the target came into view. The Skyhawks, in some excellent bombing, dropped five of the twenty-one spans. Then the formation headed for the Gulf and the haven of water. Mohrhardt, still flying a burning Crusader, got far enough to eject. A helicopter fished him out, none the worse for wear, and returned him to the "Tico." A few minutes' flying time made the difference between rescue and capture.

As the North Vietnamese air defense network evolved, it became more integrated. Originally limited to AAA around the more important targets, the system benefitted from the sporadic nature of U.S. air activity. The Communists had ample opportunity to assimilate the lessons learned along the way, to plug gaps, to react to new techniques or equipment.

Thus, the phase quickly passed when American airpower, properly employed, could have won outright air supremacy over North Viet-

nam. The navy and air force enjoyed air superiority, but only at ever-increasing cost. For as
the enemy defenses gained strength, a larger
portion of each air strike had to be devoted to
the suppression of those defenses. Crusaders
played important roles in two counter-defense
missions.

The most dangerous and least glamorous of
these was aimed at AAA and SAM activity. The
Soviet SA-2 was a 35-foot-long missile capable
of Mach 2.5 and a slant range of 25 nautical
miles. It was radar-guided, and detonated by
proximity fuze or on command, with an effective
performance envelope ranging from 1,500 to
about 63,000 feet.[9] Though SAMs brought
down a small percentage of all U.S. aircraft lost
to enemy action, the tactical environment was
largely dictated by the missiles' very existence.

Zuni rockets were widely employed against
AAA batteries, missile sites, and radar tracking
stations that controlled such threats. But tackling
the guns and SAMs was seldom an either/or
proposition. The missiles rendered medium-
and high-altitude flight unacceptably hazardous,
especially in marginal weather. The SAMs performed best in the upper reaches of their pa-
rameters where radar guidance was most effective.

Therefore, SAMs were best defeated by
flying low, where search and target radars were
partially blind. Rapid, violent evasive maneuvers
within 3,000 feet of the ground gave the missiles
little chance to track an aircraft. But the chilling
battle for survival was far from won by evading
the SAMs. And the North Vietnamese well knew
it. For the very act of dropping down under the
radar coverage placed an aircraft well within the
effective range of antiaircraft artillery. With 23-
mm to 100-mm guns, firing under radar guidance or local control, "Triple A" constituted a
pilot's worst enemy. Carefully sited batteries, fir-

97

ing barrages of patterned salvos, accounted for some 85 percent of all U.S. aircraft losses over the North.

Crusaders played a brutally delicate game of decoy in the continuing battle against the SAMs. Electronic countermeasures could confuse or defeat some of the missiles, and most tactical aircraft had their own ECM capability. Other planes dedicated to ECM—EA-3s and EA-6s—took on the full-time responsibility. And the sporty little Skyhawks carrying Shrike anti-radar missiles on "Iron Hand" duty lent their support in destroying radar sites. But the SAMs were always active to some degree. Inevitably, the missiles were fired and pilots had to contend with them.

The most vulnerable aircraft were the strike birds: A-4s, A-6s, A-7s, and frequently F-4s. Heavily laden with external stores, they lacked the agility to turn tightly or sustain high G loads in prolonged evasive action. Moreover, the attack pilots had to concentrate on hitting the target. If they were distracted by SAM warnings or the eerie glow of a missile closing on them, their accuracy naturally declined. And if forced to jettison their ordnance, even if they returned home, the opposition had won that round.

So in 1966 the F-8 squadrons began a dicey dance with the SAMs, a swirling, violent contest as complex as twentieth-century technology and yet as simple as a child's game of tag. The concept probably originated with VF-162 aboard the *Oriskany*. Commander Richard M. Bellinger of the Hunter squadron correctly figured that the defenders had no way of identifying U.S. aircraft types on radar. He also believed that sending a two-plane section above and ahead of the strike force would induce the SAM battery commanders to concentrate on their best target. If so, the attacking divisions could get to their target with little or no missile threat.

The Vietnamese seldom exhibited much fire discipline with SAMs or AAA. The Soviets and Chinese kept them well supplied with ammunition and missiles, and most batteries seemed trigger-happy. SAMs were often fired in pairs, but salvos of ten to fifteen were not unknown. This predilection could be worked to the advantage of the fliers. If the defenders shot their wad in trying to bag two or four F-8 decoys, there would be precious little remaining to shoot at the more vulnerable Skyhawks, Intruders, and Corsairs.

Bellinger and his wingman put the theory to the ultimate empirical test. Flying ahead of a strike group, the two Crusaders popped up near the target, simulating preparation for a diving attack. The SAM radars glowed with a distinct blip, and Bellinger was pleasured with the immediate attention of eight missiles.

The Crusaders were "clean wing" for this exacting mission. Devoid of external stores, they were unhindered in airspeed or maneuverability. Therefore, when the SAMs launched, Bellinger and his number two could yank and bank to their hearts' content. In a series of oppressive, mind-numbing maneuvers, they dived and turned, boomed and braked, until the last of the missiles had passed. It was an extremely busy few minutes, not only flying the Crusaders to the limit of their performance, but keeping track of multiple SAMs at the same time.

But it worked. The strike birds got to their target without one missile fired their way. Dueling an inanimate object at speeds close to Mach 1, with loads of five to eight Gs, is a soul-wrenching experience. A few pilots have likened it to the sensation a sailor feels when watching a torpedo churning toward his ship. But a torpedo is comparatively indiscriminate. It is fired at a large vessel, and travels at perhaps 50 knots. A SAM, on the other hand, as seen from the cock-

99

pit, is aimed directly at the pilot, eating up the distance at 1,800 mph. An aviator's skill and alertness will determine whether he lives or dies.

So went the Crusader's long war against ground defenses. The second suppressive mission assigned F-8s was far more popular and much better publicized. It was the fighter pilot's bread-and-butter: seeking, engaging, and destroying enemy interceptors. Crusader combats with MiGs are detailed in chapter six, but a brief examination is warranted here.

The North Vietnamese Air Force relied almost exclusively on MiG-17s and -21s. Though the former was of immediate post–Korean War vintage, it was widely considered the more dangerous opponent. This was chiefly due to its maneuverability. The -21 was as fast as most U.S. aircraft and relied mainly on heat-seeking missiles for armament. But the -17, with a gun or missile option and a cut-and-thrust fighting technique, was more versatile. Outright speed was seldom a consideration in aerial combat; but maneuverability and acceleration were the principal ingredients of success.

Nevertheless, the dogfighting capability of the MiG-17 was in part negated by North Vietnamese tactics. They preferred hit-and-run techniques, frequently from above and astern. The Communist fighters were operated under tight ground control, and pilots were instructed by their controllers in ordinary procedures: when to jettison external fuel tanks, when to arm their missiles.

This is not to imply the MiG drivers were all dull peasants fresh from the rice paddies. Some of them were extremely proficient and aggressive. Early in the war, up to about 1966, a sizable number of the NVAF pilots were instructors from other fellow-traveling air forces. It was never officially acknowledged or widely known, but, as in Korea, it was a fact.

American aircraft flying over the North had two outside sources of information on MiG activity. These were airborne EC-121s over Laos, Lockheed Super Constellations crammed with electronics and radio gear, and fighter direction ships or carrier-based early-warning aircraft in the Tonkin Gulf. The "Super Connies" were known by their call sign, Disco, while the duty ship in the Gulf was "Red Crown."

Both sources monitored enemy radio frequencies and plotted unidentified or hostile aircraft for the benefit of U.S. pilots. Therefore, up until 1966 or so, the air-ground transmissions emanating from North Vietnam were frequently Korean or Russian. Reports of East German pilots in Vietnam are unverifiable. It stands to reason that some Red Chinese controllers or pilots may have been involved, but the Vietnamese have historically shunned Chinese influence, hence the dominance of Korean and Russian advisors.

MiGs were generally fair game for American fighters, when positive identification was made— but only in the air, for the first two years or so. Grounded MiGs were immune to attack until 1967, for political reasons. As it was known that Soviet personnel were directing and sometimes flying MiGs, the Johnson administration sought to reduce the risk to Russians in much the same fashion as it did to SAMs and shipping. Air force and navy pilots recall flying in low over the airfields ringing Hanoi, seeing MiGs lined up on the runway, and passing without firing a shot. Those MiGs were then safe to take off behind the U.S. formations, in excellent position to attack.

At one point, circa 1966, Robert McNamara was asked why MiGs remained immune to attack on the ground. The secretary of defense replied that if enemy fighters were destroyed on their bases, the Vietnamese would simply move the

101

A VFP-63 photo bird completes a roll around a four-plane division of A-6A Intruders. The Crusader's four cameras would enable an all-aspect view of the formation. (Peter B. Mersky)

bases farther north, perhaps into China. This was apparently the official explanation, without any public mention of Soviet participation, as it made absolutely no sense tactically. Moving the MiGs north would only have benefitted American aviators by reducing the expanded net of NVN fighter airfields, and putting the MiGs farther from their operating areas. Nevertheless, it was at this point that U.S. pilots began drawing conclusions on the aptness of Robert Strange McNamara's middle name.

Crusaders performed two functions in dealing with MiGs: escorting strike and reconnaissance aircraft, and patrolling assigned sectors in hopes of engaging MiGs on their way to intercept U.S. formations. The latter fell under the broad heading of Combat Air Patrol, with specific functions such as Target CAP or MiGCAP, sometimes characterized as "trolling for MiGs." TarCAPS were assigned stations near a designated target to shortstop incoming bandits, while MiGCAPS had more of a free-lance mission.

Coordination between MiGs and ground defenses allowed the MiGs to be employed as decoys. The World War II phrase was "flak bait," but the same principle applied with SAMs and AAA. If an eager American fighter jock ignored air discipline or lost his judgment in the heat of a chase, he stood in peril of following a MiG into a thicket of missiles and antiaircraft guns. So MiGs could pose a threat in passive as well as active roles.

Photo escorts generally involved one fighter covering an RF-8. On these missions, the recon aircraft usually flew at 4,000 feet above ground level with the fighter split wide at four o'clock or eight o'clock in "loose deuce" formation. At 4,000 the planes were above the effective fire of light-caliber guns, and low enough to take quick evasive maneuvers in the event of a SAM launch. But there was no getting around the medium and heavy flak, and since anything worth photographing was likely well defended, the best way to get the job done was to get in, get the pictures, and get out—fast.

It didn't always work. Except for one cruise by Airlant's VFP-62, the only light photographic squadron involved in the navy's air war over the North was VFP-63, based at NAS Miramar near San Diego. "Fightin' Photo" kept detachments at sea almost continuously from 1964 to 1973, and suffered a loss rate three times the navy average. The reason was terrifyingly simple. In order to get the photos, the RF-8 had to maintain a constant course and altitude. This worked heavily in favor of AAA gunners, whose tracking solution was vastly simplified when the target flew straight and level. Entering and exiting the target area, the photo pilot could take evasive action, but once committed to his run, he could only sit there, bend the throttle, and hope.

During the war, VFP-63 lost twenty RF-8Gs, almost a quarter of total Crusader losses to enemy action. Eight of the pilots were rescued, seven were killed, and five taken prisoner, spending long years in harsh confinement at POW camps given such innocuous nicknames as the "Hanoi Hilton" or the "Plantation." If the North Vietnamese were stubborn, committed, and resourceful, they were also brutal captors, frequently more interested in extracting prop-aganda statements from prisoners than infor-mation. Treatment of POWs improved after 1970, though many downed fliers had spent four or five years in prison by that time.

A seldom-used option on photo Crusaders was the underwing sensor pod and long instrument boom. (Peter B. Mersky)

Still, some pilots seemed to thrive on risk. Captain James Morgan, an air force exchange pilot with VFP-63, flew two tours in Vietnam for a total of 166 combat missions. The standard air force tour was 100 missions over the North, and Morgan's record represents additional shakes of the dice by a factor of two-thirds.

For over three years—from 1968 to 1971— photo-recon flights constituted the majority of American aircraft sorties into North Vietnamese airspace. In March 1968 the Johnson administration halted bombing above the nineteenth parallel, sparing the upper 60 percent of North Vietnam from air attack. This was followed in November by Johnson's announcement of a complete bombing halt in hopes of engaging the Communists in the Paris "peace talks."

While the delegates talked about the shape of the conference table and the Nixon-Kissinger administration took over, recon flights continued. The basis for these flights was presumably misunderstood or tacitly ignored by one or both sides. Under the "understanding" that Henry Kissinger established, unarmed recon flights could continue. But the North Vietnamese continued to shoot at recce aircraft, without penalty.

This situation eventually led to the policy of "protective reaction" strikes, an innocuous phrase that thinly covered retaliatory attacks against troublesome flak or SAM batteries. Presumably the North Vietnamese agreed that unarmed aircraft would not be fired upon, but American pilots were allowed to defend themselves. Since the only authorized U.S. aircraft over the North at this time were required to be unarmed, just how they could shoot back seems uncertain. In these matters, Richard Nixon and Henry Kissinger seemed no more astute than their predecessors.

In any event, retaliatory air attacks were made against specific AAA and SAM sites. When field commanders were accused (in some cases accurately) of using the "protective reaction" option beyond the spirit of the "understanding," it became a matter of public debate. The affair was thrashed out in Congress, the Pentagon, and the news media amid charges, countercharges, denials, and finally reprimands for some ranking officers.

Meanwhile, the men in RF-8 cockpits continued to get shot at. Crusader fighters were reduced to "riding shotgun" with empty chambers. Not even 20-mm ammunition was allowed. Thus, the only reason escorting F-8s still accompanied recon aircraft was that if one were shot down, the survivor could hope to return to tell the tale.

Following the bombing halt above the seventeenth parallel, F-8 squadrons flew substantially more BarCAPS and photo escorts than before, while coastal recces remained about the same, but strikes were almost nonexistent. Lieutenant Tom Weinel, flying F-8Js off the *Oriskany* in 1969, spoke for many Crusader "drivers" when he said, "It was a hell of a dull war for a fighter pilot."[10]

Whether operating before or after the bombing halt, procedures were generally the same. Escort missions usually involved "Alpha strikes," major efforts mounted by each air wing, sometimes in concert with planes from another carrier. The *Essex*-class ships generally embarked two F-8 squadrons, two A-4 squadrons, and an A-1 outfit. An Alpha strike from one of these air wings customarily involved over two dozen aircraft: twelve Skyhawk bombers and two A-4 Iron Hands to deal with enemy radar sites; a four-plane Crusader division for TarCAP; and four more assigned to flak suppression. Bringing up the rear was a photo section, including a fighter escort, for damage assessment.

Additionally, two or three KA-3 Skywarrior tankers would rendezvous for in-flight refueling, and perhaps a couple of "wet wing" A-4s with buddy pack fuel tanks. The prop-driven A-1s provided ResCAP in the event of a strike aircraft going down, and another division of F-8s sometimes went along on MiGCAP. But the latter Crusaders seldom accompanied the strike; they took station wherever the MiG threat was most likely to develop.

"Mini Alphas" were also flown against smaller targets. Four A-4s were squired to the target by two to four F-8s on TarCAP and flak suppression. This allowed a compact, flexible formation to get in and out without drawing undue attention. At least that was the intent.

Most of the early navy strikes against the Thanh Hoa Bridge were mini-Alphas. Some pilots returned shaking their heads, having watched their ordnance bounce off the immense structure. After a while, humorists took note of the situation. There was a famous cartoon circulated during the war, showing the planet Earth crumbling apart, with the "Dragon's Jaw" remaining intact.

Regardless of the size of the strike, the mission sequence followed similar patterns. Pilots launched from perhaps 130 miles offshore, linked up, and headed west. Usually they plugged in to the tankers before proceeding inland. Then, tanks topped off, they dispersed into tactical formation. By this time the opposition generally knew something was brewing. Soviet merchant vessels and Vietnamese fishing boats plied the waters of the Tonkin Gulf undisturbed, since a state of war did not officially exist. They duly reported the composition and direction of the carrier aircraft before any blips appeared on a Vietnamese radarscope.

With "feet dry" over the coast, the first tentative warnings of enemy radar became evident.

107

The strike aircraft sometimes remained low over the multihued greenish-brown rice paddies and brilliant green jungle, but they were tracked nonetheless. However, the North Vietnamese radars never dared remain locked on for long. They briefly came "up," tracking for a few seconds, before shutting down. The Iron Hands, with Shrike radar-homing missiles, escorted strikes for just that purpose.

Additionally, ECM aircraft monitored hostile radar frequencies. The ECM operators could tell if the enemy were tracking "with curiosity" or "with intent." In the former instance, a brief scanning signal was employed. But if a SAM or AAA battery were tracking long enough to gain a firing solution, it was evident. For this reason, many antiaircraft guns were fired under manual control. They were less accurate than the radar-guided weapons, but they were also free of sudden retaliation in the form of a Shrike landing in their midst.

Excellent targets were spread the length of North Vietnam, but a majority were found in the upper portion of the country, where supplies and communications were concentrated. For American aviators, Hanoi was "Downtown," the embodiment of Petula Clark's 1965 hit song that promised that Downtown was where "everything's waiting for you." And so it was: AAA, SAMs, and MiGs.

The SAM warnings came faster as ECM gear picked up the intermittent radar emissions, or visual sightings told of missiles fired under local control. The formations loosened up some more, giving each pilot maneuvering room as the strike leaders coached their troops. "Heads up, now. SAMs being launched. Spread it out a little. There's a sighting. . . . OK, take it down, take it down. . . ."

Far more often than not, the missiles were evaded or defeated by countermeasures. But the triple A could be anywhere—and usually was. With advance notice of the probable target, mobile flak batteries were rolled into position and waiting when the attackers arrived. Then the sky was laced with streaks of tracers and erupting bursts of fuzed shells. Most common were the 37- and 57-mm guns, sometimes in multiple mounts, firing either pattern or salvo. At the target, the F-8s dived ahead to take out the most troublesome batteries with Zunis and gunfire while the A-4s or A-7s popped up, rolled in, and released their ordnance.

Then it was time to get out, as low as they dared, heading for the coast. And all too frequently there came the eerie, haunting, high-pitched bleeps of an emergency beacon. Somebody had been hit and punched out, activating his beeper. Then the A-1s move in, the prop-driven "Spads" that could loiter at low level far longer than any jet, helping to locate and protect

The family resemblance is obvious as a Vought A-7A Corsair II undergoes carrier trials by the Naval Air Test Center with a Crusader sharing the deck. In the 1980s LTV proposed the A-7X, remanufactured to provide performance comparable to the F-8. However, the F/A-18 Hornet became the Navy's new strike fighter. (Peter B. Mersky)

the downed flier until a rescue helicopter arrived. Crusaders, with their 20-mm guns, could also perform the ResCap role, but not without frequent detours to the offshore tankers to refill their fuel tanks.

The heaviest losses suffered by a carrier air wing in one WestPac deployment were sustained by CVW-16 during the 1967–68 *Oriskany* cruise. The air wing included two Crusader squadrons: VF-111 with Charlies and VF-162 with Echoes. In the first line period, from 12 July to 7 August, the "Mighty O" lost fourteen aircraft to all causes: eight A-4s, four F-8s, an A-1, and a KA-3. Eight aviators were killed, missing, or taken prisoner in that twenty-six-day period.

It only got worse. By the end of the tour in mid-January 1968, Air Wing 16 had spent 124 days on the line, losing thirty-eight planes, twenty-one pilots, and six aircrewmen. These figures should be compared to the nominal complement of seventy aircraft and ninety pilots in an *Essex*-class air wing. Thus, CVW-16 had sustained aircraft losses of 54 percent and pilot losses of 23 percent of authorized strength. However, of the thirty-eight aircraft lost to all causes, sixteen pilots were rescued from the water or from enemy soil.

Six aviators were captured: three Crusader and three Skyhawk pilots, one of whom died in captivity. Another A-4 pilot probably would have survived in prison, but never had the chance. Hit by a SAM over Haiphong in August, he ejected safely but was killed by antiaircraft gunners who fired on his parachute.

Nine of the aircraft losses were indirectly related to combat, including an F-8C on launch. Two Skyhawks disappeared over North Vietnam in unknown circumstances. Of the twenty-seven known combat losses (seventeen A-4Es, five F-8Cs, four F-8Es, and an A-1H), twenty-one fell to AAA and six to SAMs. The two Crusader squadrons were typical, losing a total of seven F-8s to flak and two to SAMs.

Air Wing 16 had already sustained crippling losses during the previous tour. In October 1966 a hangar-deck fire had killed forty-four men. This, combined with combat attrition, meant the loss of 40 percent of the air wing personnel. After two dicey back-to-back deployments, the survivors were sent to shore duty for a full year.

So went the repetitious cycle of strikes, escorts, recons, and flak suppression. In turn, they became deployments with retraining and redeployment for eight years. The record among Crusader-equipped air wings was held by CVW-19, with eight cruises between 1964 and 1973. The two F-8 squadrons were VF-191 and 194, flying Echoes and Juliets from the *Bon Homme Richard*, *Ticonderoga*, and *Oriskany*. On its third tour, Air Wing 19 spent 120 days on the line from October 1966 to May 1967. In that period, Satan's Kittens of 191 logged over 1,000 combat sorties from the *Ticonderoga* for an aggregate of over 3,000 hours in F-8Es. They expended some 23,000 rounds of 20-mm ammo, over 300 Zunis, and almost 100 tons of bombs.[11]

Close behind was Air Wing 21, with seven WestPac cruises from 1964 to 1972. The *Hancock* and "Bonny Dick" were the flattops from which VF-24 and 211 flew F-8C, E, H, and J Crusaders. And flew them superbly well. For these were the MiG killers, with a dozen victories between them. At the time of the 1968 bombing halt, the Checkertails and Checkmates had accounted for 40 percent of all MiGs shot down by navy aircraft.

One of the VF-211 pilots was Lieutenant Cole Pierce, who flew from both the *Hancock* and *Bon Homme Richard*. His logbook offers a detailed examination of the relative roles performed by the Crusader and Phantom, as he returned to combat flying F-4s off the *America* in VF-74 during 1972–73. The following breakdown consol-

Crusaders and Skyhawks of Hancock's Air Wing 21 join an Air Force KC-135 over the Tonkin Gulf in 1972. (Harrison)

idates all CAP missions, be they Target, Force, Barrier, or MiG patrol, and similarly lumps together armed recon and strike sorties.

	VF-211 in 1967 (F-8s)	VF-74 in 1972–73 (F-4s)
Combat Air Patrols	61%	48%
Armed Recon/Strikes	12%	43%
Photo Escort	11%	3%
Flak Suppression	10%	1%
Weather Reconnaissance	6%	1%
Close Air Support	0%	3%

As the war entered its final phase in the spring of 1972, the aviators flying over the North were astonished at the change. When the Nixon administration finally decided to employ its military option, the impact was dramatic. By mining Haiphong and other ports, and reopening the bombing campaign against North Vietnamese transportation, aerial supremacy was established. Henry Kissinger had been given nearly three years to charm the Communists into a settlement, and he failed. Tactical and strategic airpower accomplished that goal in a few months.

With their outside sources of supply largely cut off, the North Vietnamese soon used up most of their firepower. The MiGs were gleefully hunted down and destroyed or driven from the air by navy and air force F-4s. In seven months of intense activity, Phantoms shot down some seventy-five MiGs—nearly as many as had been bagged in all of 1967. The Thanh Hoa and Paul Doumer bridges were toppled by "smart bombs" in May, and the attacking aircraft escaped without loss or damage.

Cole Pierce was typical of the pilots who noted the difference in the aftermath of renewed air operations. The comparison of NVN antiair defenses from the end of his previous Tonkin Gulf tour and the time of his return in 1972 was, he said, "astounding." He recalls in detail: "SAM activity was less than a quarter of what it had been. It was really unusual to encounter SAMs over North Vietnam in latter 1972 into early 1973, where before it was unusual not to meet SAMs. The AAA activity was likewise reduced, being very weak and ineffective. Our tactics had not appreciably changed, so I can only surmise that their logistics and manpower had suffered greatly. An aircraft returning with battle damage was commonplace in 1967–69, but it would draw a crowd on the flight deck in '72. MiG activity was similarly reduced. Air Wing 21 left the line for the U.S. in August

1967 having shot down as many MiGs as the rest of the navy put together. But our air wing aboard the *America* in '72 had only three engagements over a ten-month period."[12]

Toward the end, U.S. intelligence estimated that there were perhaps no more than two dozen SAMs left in North Vietnam. The 57-, 85-, and 100-mm AA guns had fallen silent for lack of ammunition. These were the weapons that had claimed the majority of American aircraft previously, but now enemy gunners were reduced to banging away with 23-mm "popguns."

From January 1964 to January 1973, seven carrier air wings made a total of twenty-nine Vietnam cruises with ten F-8 squadrons, not counting forty VFP-63 detachments. These ten fighter squadrons made fifty-five individual WestPac deployments during those years, usually with two Crusader squadrons per carrier.

Of the five F-8 fighter versions that flew over Vietnam, Echoes and Juliets were by far the most numerous. Eight squadrons made a total of twenty-two deployments with F-8Es, while seven flew F-8Js on nineteen deployments. Three squadrons operated F-8 Charlies during seven trips, and four squadrons accounted for six deployments with Hotels. The lone F-8D unit in combat was VF-154 in 1965, whose cruise in the *Coral Sea* made the Black Knights the only Crusader squadron engaged in combat from other than an *Essex*-class ship.

Combat attrition among F-8s was neither the highest nor the lowest of the war. From 1964 to 1973 inclusive, eighty-three Crusaders were stricken from the record, destroyed or damaged beyond repair (DBR) by enemy action. Another 109 required major rebuilds, for a total of 192 F-8 casualties. Over three-quarters of these were carrier-based, with seventy-one "strikes" and eighty-nine "majors." The remaining thirty-two were marine Crusaders based in South Vietnam.

Of these, a dozen were shot down, destroyed on the ground, or DBR.

By way of comparison, Phantom losses among navy and marine squadrons totaled 141 destroyed or DBR, and 180 with major damage. Of these 321 casualties, nearly half were land-based F-4s, reflecting the marines' greater use of Phantoms in-country. It is also noteworthy that in the eight months of 1973 before American involvement completely ended, thirteen Phantoms were written off and eighteen received major damage. During the same period, F-8 casualties involved one stricken and one with major damage—ample indication of the Crusader's reduced activity.

The ratio of aircraft written off in relation to the total receiving disabling or fatal damage was nearly identical for Crusaders and Phantoms: 43 percent and 44 percent respectively. Furthermore, it was substantially the same for both types operating off carriers: 44 percent for Crusaders and 45 percent among Phantoms. The ratios of "strikes" while in South Vietnam were slightly different, with 37 percent of marine F-8 casualties compared to 43 percent of marine F-4s. However, among aircraft hit on the ground in mortar or artillery barrages, no comparison may be drawn as to their relative merits.

At first glance it appears that the twin-engine Phantom did no better in surviving major battle damage than its single-engine counterpart. But a definition of terms is probably required. An F-4 that lost one engine to light-caliber flak could still limp home and never appear in the statistics of aircraft suffering major damage. An engine change is a relatively simple, routine affair. But an F-8 sustaining the same type of damage automatically became a loss in most circumstances. Thus, the Crusader comes off very well indeed in comparison to its bigger, better-publicized teammate.

115

For the F-8 squadrons, the 1972–73 denouement proved somehow disappointing. They had very few MiG encounters, and provided yeoman service in the roles they had always performed: flak suppression, photo escort, and barrier or force CAP. At the end in January 1973, Air Wing 19 with VF-191 and 194 aboard the *Oriskany* was the only unit with Crusaders still active in WestPac as fighters.

Like the pilots and crews of other aircraft, the F-8 community knew it had won a victory over North Vietnam. Many—perhaps most— also knew that that victory would be thrown away, sapped by a lack of national willpower and the previous years of indecision by two presidential administrations. When the willingness finally took hold, it was far too late to recover whatever momentum had existed years before.

Attainment of aerial supremacy over the North amounted to a tactical victory on a grand scale. But it was not so much an end of a troubled journey as a stopping place along the way, where America got off and watched the train of defeat continue to its inevitable destination. It allowed a president to speak of peace with honor, and for his secretary of state to accept a Nobel Prize for a peace that never existed. Meanwhile, many good men had died for nothing. There can be no more damning indictment of any war.

MiG Encounters

6

Nobody would claim the Crusader was the best-known aircraft of the Vietnam War. That distinction probably belongs to McDonnell Douglas's F-4 Phantom or Bell's ubiquitous UH-1 helicopter, the hard-working Huey. But if the F-8 gained a popular image, it was the cultivated reputation of the lone gunfighter. Wartime accounts and quasi-official news releases made repeated mention of the Crusader's 20-mm cannon as the reason behind its exceptional success in air combat. "MiG Master," they called it, the inference being that the guns were responsible.

In a sense they were—but only indirectly. The fact remains that of nineteen MiGs credited to Crusaders, only two were destroyed solely with gunfire. In two other instances, F-8 pilots finished off damaged MiGs following a missile attack by using their 20-mm guns. But the AIM-9 was the Crusader's primary weapon. Why and how the situation evolved, and the dispelling of a legend, is part of the Crusader story.

During the early 1960s, naval aviation emphasized fleet defense. Planners envisioned big-war scenarios in which interceptors scrambled from carrier decks to engage hostile bombers threatening the task force. This concept had considerable validity, particularly in the Mediterranean. Therefore, Demons and Phantoms (McDonnell was always big on spooks) were armed with Sparrows, augmented by Sidewinders, for long-range air defense. The F3H, with four 20-mm guns to boot, was the most potent fighter of its time, but never saw a day of combat.

With the arrival of supersonic interceptors and radar-guided missiles, dogfights were presumably a thing of the past. But astute aviators knew that increasing airspeeds were supposed to bring the demise of dogfighting before World War II, when all-metal monoplanes became standard equipment. The same claim had been made with the advent of jets, but the Korean War proved it false.

The same thing happened in Vietnam. The U.S. Air Force and Navy were geared up to fight a war that never came. Of the American aircraft that flew regularly over the North from 1965 on, only the F-8 could be called a true air-superiority fighter. The F-4 series was heavily committed to the strike role, and the navy never installed a gun in the Phantom. The air force hung gun pods on some F-4s, and by the end of 1967 had an internal 20-mm gatling in the F-4E. But regardless of their branch of service, Phantoms remained multimission aircraft.

Similarly, the F-105 was never intended as anything but a fighter-bomber. However, the Thunderchief gave a good account of itself, being built with an internal 20-mm that was used effectively against MiGs. In fact, 105s accounted for one-fifth of all airforce shootdowns. And of the 137 MiGs credited to all air force pilots, forty (or 29 percent) were achieved in whole or in part with 20-mm fire. The navy's ratio was only about 10 percent wholly or partially with guns: four by Crusaders and two by A-1s.

Therefore, a curious anomaly arose. Crusaders seldom fired their guns in air combat, but the very fact that they had those four 20-mm guns provided a peacetime training stimulus to remain proficient in air combat maneuvering. Neither the rest of the navy, nor the air force, devoted much attention to fighter-versus-fighter combat in pre-war training.

True, there were hot-rod aircraft in the navy inventory—mainly the sporty little F4D and the nimble F11F—but they were produced in limited numbers. Like the Demon, they were never placed in a combat environment, so their potential and adaptability were never fully tested.

Meanwhile, most American fighter pilots were becoming either interceptor pilots or fighter-bomber pilots. The distinctions may seem narrow to outsiders, but they are as different as Grand Prix racing is from sports-car rallying or Indianapolis racing.

Briefly, interceptors such as the F-102/106 family in the air force or F4Ds in the navy were meant to deal with enemy bombers. A fast rate of climb and long-range detection, with missile weapons, were called for. On the other hand, fighter-bombers generally operated at much lower altitude, dividing their attention between tactical air support and an air-combat capability. Pure fighters—aircraft designed and equipped to engage their own kind to determine who owns any specific cube of contested airspace—were increasingly rare. Interceptors and fighter-bombers can each successfully perform the ACM role, but not as well as an aircraft dedicated solely to that mission. This was the difference between the F-8 and every other American aircraft that operated over North Vietnam.

Therefore, many F-8 squadrons—perhaps most of them—remained proficient at aerial combat. Those four 20-mm guns were a prime reason. The unreliable, pesky, frustrating cannon caused some squadrons maintenance heartaches, but the guns were *there*. It was difficult to completely ignore them. And since the Crusader was originally designed as an uncompromised air-superiority fighter, with a clean wing and little strike potential, the F-8 community tended to remain ACM-oriented. Of course, the underwing hardpoints eventually came, but the prewar attitude remained. Crusader pilots were *fighter* jocks, by God, with no ifs, ands, or hyphens.

It is often said that a fighter pilot's job is deliciously simple: shoot down the opposition. Actually, that is a popular simplification. The fighter's main role has always been control of the air. Whether that aim is achieved in actual combat, or simply by intimidating the enemy with a superior show of force, matters little. The fighter exists to provide its own bombers, reconnaissance, and transport aircraft a safe operating environment. Of course, the achievement of that goal frequently involves shooting the other fellow out of the sky. And for seven decades it has been the most glamorous of all military occupations.

The Crusader performed this usually well-respected role in the least popular and probably worst-managed war in American history. But the F-8's starring role in its career occurred relatively early, in the first half of the Vietnam War. The broader history of the Crusader's participation was dealt with in the previous chapter. What follows is an examination of the "gunfighter's" specialty—aerial combat.

Crusaders shot down eighteen MiGs between June 1966 and September 1968. The victories occurred during twelve engagements, with peak periods in June 1966, May and July 1967, and June and July of 1968. These were the months of the best flying weather.

Those hassles that resulted in MiG kills followed a reasonably consistent pattern. The successful engagements occurred during strike or photo escorts, though roving MiGCap flights that accompanied Alpha strikes were also rewarded with shootdowns. In short, the MiGs displayed little ambition to mix it with lone sections or divisions of fighters. They were after bombers or photo planes.

In every instance where adequate data is available, the F-8 combats occurred entirely below 10,000 feet; most were well below that level. This was a factor of the overall North Vietnamese antiair network. SAMs and triple A dictated low-level tactics that put the American aircraft below most of the radar cover and complicated the SAMs' guidance. There was no escaping the flak until the blockade began taking effect in 1972. It was something that aviators came to live with.

Few F-8 pilots began a successful MiG combat with an altitude advantage. Some engagements were initiated on the same level as the bandit, but by far the majority started with MiGs on top. As we have seen, the hostile tactical environment denied U.S. aircraft access to the higher altitudes.

Another factor was relative numbers. Though the combined U.S. Navy and Air Force strength far outweighed North Vietnam's, most Crusaders-versus-MiG encounters occurred with approximately equal odds. This remained a fairly consistent factor throughout the war. Not even a majority of total American aircraft could be committed at any one time, and those that were concentrated in a target area usually operated in twos and fours. Therefore, the chances of one side or the other gaining significant numerical advantage in a localized area were small. In most instances where F-8s outnumbered MiGs, the odds were two on one.

Therefore, all things considered, the North Vietnamese interceptors began with a huge ad-

121

vantage. They possessed the traditional trump card in the game of aerial combat—altitude— and could often strike when and wherever they desired. In actuality, their GCI controllers made these decisions, but it amounted to the same thing if one were on the receiving end. Furthermore, the MiGs had large numbers of targets and repeated opportunities—ideal circumstances for building fat scores.

In every major air war in history, the outnumbered air force has produced the most successful individual pilots: the Germans in World War I, the Axis powers in World War II, the Americans in Korea, the Israelis in the Middle East, and the Pakistanis against the Indians in 1965 and 1971. The trend continued in Vietnam. At least nine MiG pilots were credited with five or more American aircraft, and while details are understandably lacking, it appears they engaged air force planes more often than those of the navy.

By contrast, only two Americans became aces in Vietnam: one air force and one navy. Both flew Phantoms in the peak period of MiG activity during 1972. While direct comparisons are misleading owing to the different circumstances, a quick look at Korea and Vietnam indicates how things had changed in fifteen years. From 1950 to 1953, forty U.S. fighter pilots achieved ace status, all but one in F-86 Sabres. The overall victory-loss ratio in air combat was tagged at fourteen to one. Discounting the three-year halt in the air offensive over North Vietnam, a similar period of combat was waged from 1965 to 1972. By the time of the early 1973 settlement, the U.S. Air Force and Navy had to settle for a wartime exchange rate of barely two to one.

Some similarities existed, however. Korea was a flight commander's war, as four aircraft were usually the most that could be controlled in a combat. The Vietnam experience tended to confirm this aspect of jet fighter operations, and if anything furthered the trend. If Korea was a flight leader's war, Vietnam was a section leader's war. Few MiG engagements involved more than a leader and wingman on either side, for reasons already mentioned. And since the leader invariably got the first shot, relatively few number twos bagged a MiG over North Vietnam.

The fourteen-to-one kill ratio in Korea has come in for close scrutiny in recent years, and estimates have reduced the actual figure to something closer to eight to one. But even allowing for the historical factor of two kills for every three claimed, it is clear that American fighters did far better in Korea than in Vietnam. The reasons are painful to recall.

For much of the war, air strikes into North Vietnam were run by "remote control" from Washington—frequently by DOD or State Department civilians. Routes and timing were often repeated as if the Pentagon were running an airline instead of a bombing campaign, and predictability in war only simplifies the enemy's task. It was incompetent at best, criminally negligent at worst, but it worked to the benefit of the MiGs. They had little difficulty locating their targets, waiting for the opportune moment, then striking in swift hit-and-run attacks.

It was said that no truly professional American fighter pilot would not have cheerfully traded places with a MiG driver. Air force Colonel Robin Olds, CO of the famed Eighth Tactical Fighter Wing, held the American record for nearly five years with his four confirmed kills. But Olds said he liked to think that, if roles were reversed, he'd have shot down fifty U.S. aircraft.[1]

Offsetting the North Vietnamese advantages were superior American experience and flying skill. Among F-8 squadrons in combat

123

prior to 1969, even the most junior pilots probably had 500 to 800 hours of Crusader time. The division leaders, including squadron COs and execs, frequently had 3,000 hours or more in their logbooks, of which over half was usually spent in F-8s. It is extremely unlikely that any North Vietnamese pilots approached these totals, though some North Koreans or Russians might have. But a good many MiG drivers had spent fewer than 300 hours in the air, total time.

Longer experience and the tactical advantages of leadership positions showed up among MiG killers. Of the eighteen Crusader pilots who bagged a MiG prior to 1969, fully one-third were commanders and five were lieutenant commanders. Four were bull lieutenants, while only three "jaygees" scored a kill.

The Crusader itself possessed some important advantages over the opposition. F-8s generally had better visibility from the cockpit, a far superior fire-control system, more varied armament, and a wider performance envelope than Communist fighters. Both combatants were proven rugged designs, capable of absorbing battle damage and returning home.

None of the MiG family, however, was as complex as its American counterparts. The Soviet design philosophy called for hardy, easily maintained fighters with simple weapons systems. They were short-legged, hard-turning dogfighters that traced their ancestry back to the 1940 collaboration of Russian designers Mikoyan and Gurevich. When flown by the numbers, under close control from the ground, they could be effectively flown by relative amateurs.

The MiGs encountered in Vietnam came in three varieties: models -17, -19, and -21. The MiG-17 has served in at least twenty fellow-traveling air forces around the world since its operational debut in 1953. It was probably the most numerous aircraft in the NVN inventory, for over half of all MiG kills were -17s.

NATO's code name for the -17 was Fresco, but regardless of what it was called, it packed a potent battery: a 37-mm cannon and a pair of 23-mm guns in the nose, with the option of heat-seeking Atoll missiles. However, most -17s encountered over North Vietnam were straight cannoneers. Some—not all—were equipped with afterburning engines, rated at 7,500 pounds thrust in a 13,000-pound loaded airframe.

The -17's distinctive high stabilizer was inherited from the Korean War vintage MiG-15, and in the era of infrared missiles, the Mikoyan configuration provided an unexpected benefit. From almost any angle above the MiG, that high stabilizer partially blocked the IR source, acting as a heat shield.

There were other advantages. With a wing area of some 277 square feet, the -17's wing loading was only about 47 pounds per square foot. That meant unexcelled maneuverability. If the MiG pilot were half awake, there was just no way to turn with him. Consequently, American pilots fought the -17 in the vertical most of the time, using superior speed and acceleration to gain separation and outclimb the opposition, then coming back in "yo-yo" maneuvers. Crusaders could out-turn MiGs at high airspeeds, in much the same way that Grumman F6F Hellcats outmaneuvered nimble Japanese Mitsubishi Zeroes in the Pacific during World War II. Above 200 knots, the big Grumman's superior control response remained effective, while the Mitsubishi's ailerons became semirigid under heavy aerodynamic loads. It was the same over North Vietnam. The drawback was that most jet combats occur at airspeeds under Mach 1, and F-8s could not always rely upon favorable circumstances.

125

Furthermore, a missile hit or well-aimed burst on a MiG couldn't guarantee a kill. One MiG killer, Lieutenant Commander Bobby Lee of VF-24, recalled, "For the first few years of the war we used an air-to-ground ammo combination (mostly high explosive) instead of air-to-air (armor piercing and high explosive mixed). With the former mixture we had a couple of gun engagements where the MiGs were damaged by hits in the wings and fuselage, but the HE would skin burst and not kill the engine or vital systems. The MiG is a very tough airplane."[2]

The MiG-19 was largely an also-ran in the North Vietnam air war. Never engaged in large numbers, it had generally better performance than the -17, but lacked some of the Fresco's cut-and-thrust qualities. The main armament was cannon. Only ten MiG-19s were destroyed during the war (eight by the air force and two by the navy), and apparently Crusaders seldom tangled with them.

The MiG-21 was another matter entirely. It might be considered the first truly modern fighter the Soviets produced. A British aviation writer described the Fishbed as "the most obvious aerodynamicist's design in the world." The entire design philosophy was low drag, though this in turn caused "some unpleasant structural problems."[3]

With a 25-foot wingspan—6 feet less than the -17—the MiG-21 was a sleek little jewel. Its delta wing of some 250 square feet resulted in a fairly high wing loading (on the order of 72 pounds per square foot at 18,800 pounds loaded weight), but the tradeoffs were ample. Its low structure weight, low drag, and good supersonic maneuverability were all benefits. Capable of Mach 2, the -21 was competitive with its American contemporaries, though the delta wing provided poor lift at subsonic airspeeds, where most combat occurred.

Like the Crusader, the MiG-21 possessed mixed armament as standard equipment. A pair of 30- or 37-mm guns were provided, but the main punch was two Atoll missiles, Soviet copies of the Sidewinder with a somewhat smaller motor. This was a definite improvement over earlier Russian air-to-air missiles, which were mostly "beam riders." They were guided by line-of-sight radar, which meant that if the launching aircraft were forced to break away from its target, the missile was defeated. But with the Atoll, the enemy possessed a workable heat-seeker as effective as the 'winder.

Thus, the air battles "up North" pitted two very different types of aircraft against one another: multipurpose American fighter-bombers—rather large, heavy types—against small, light, point-defense interceptors. Again, generalizations are dangerous or misleading, but combats between the American and Communist birds were usually short, intense, and often inconclusive. The ACM envelope was, as we have seen, at relatively low level, and instead of being at blinding supersonic speed, most engagements were fought at .8 Mach and less, with aircraft booming in and out of afterburner as necessary. Relatively few engagements lasted more than two or three minutes.

The scene of most air battles was the upper portion of North Vietnam, centered around Hanoi. Sixty miles up the Red River from the "hour-glass" navigational checkpoint in the coastal delta, Hanoi was protected by four main airfields. Two were very close to the capital. There was Phuc Yen about 15 miles due north, off the tip of "Thud Ridge," and Gia Lam just across the Red River to the east. Kep, probably the best-known MiG base, sat on the Northeast

Railroad leading to China, some 30 miles out of Hanoi. And Bai Thuong guarded the southern approach 65 miles out, beyond the oblong-shaped depression that the Americans called Banana Valley.

Thus, Hanoi sat in the approximate center of an ellipse that formed the main air combat arena: from roughly 30 miles northwest, where the Black River meets the Red, to Haiphong 50 miles east; and from about 70 miles south, near Thanh Hoa, to Thud Ridge 50 miles north. This oval aerial stadium, roughly the size of New Hampshire, extended from the treetops up to 20,000 feet. MiGs were chased in and out of the arena, but most aerial combats were conducted within its borders.

Whether a pilot was navy or air force, a MiG kill in his personnel file meant a lot. It brought an automatic Silver Star, usually a trip to Saigon to meet the press, with attendant interviews and publicity. Some pilots declined the honor, fearing harassment or even reprisals against their families by radicals in the States. Others preferred to keep their names unknown in case they were shot down and captured later. But the majority of MiG killers offered no objections. After the adrenalin high of a victory, something else took over. It was the more measured professional esteem they received from their colleagues. There were basically two kinds of fighter pilots in Korea and Vietnam—those with MiGs and those without. Those who had 'em enjoyed a status that neither rank nor decorations could match.

Aerial combat began over North Vietnam in the spring of 1965. On 3 April, the *Coral Sea* and *Hancock* launched a combined strike of fifty planes against an important bridge south of Hanoi. The A-4s dropped a span, while two carrier planes were lost to AAA. But during the

same mission, some MiGs made one quick, ineffective gunnery run and sped away. That was
the first aerial encounter of the war. Next day
the MiGs improved their performance. They
slipped up on an F-105 formation attacking
Thanh Hoa Bridge and quickly shot down two
Thuds.

By the middle of June, North Vietnam possessed some seventy MiGs—reportedly -15s and
-17s. The first -21s didn't arrive until year-end,
but in the meantime the older models kept busy.
Two F-4Bs of VF-21 scored the first U.S. victories of the war on 17 June, knocking down a
pair of -17s. Three days later a *Midway* A-1 pilot
splashed another -17 that foolishly flew in front
of his Skyraider.

Air Force Phantoms bagged a brace of -17s
on 10 July, and then things let up for three
months. In October a Fighting 151 F-4 got the
navy's fourth kill. But the on-again, off-again
nature of the war, combined with poor weather,
reduced air combat to zero for the next five
months. Then in April of 1966 the air force ran
wild, knocking down six MiGs, plus another in
May. It brought the American box score to thirteen kills in thirteen months.

As yet, Crusaders had no more than some
sightings. But when the *Hancock* returned to the
line on 7 June for a second tour, Air Wing 21
intended to change all that. The new CAG was
Commander Jack Monger, a longtime attack
pilot who replaced an experienced fighter jock
as air wing commander. At the change of command ceremony, Monger had astonished the
fighter pilots by saying, "We will get MiGs."[4]

One of the two F-8 squadrons was VF-211,
led by Commander Harold L. Marr. A balding,
thirty-nine-year-old Oregonian, Marr was eager
to tangle with the MiGs, but nobody in his squadron had ever seen one. His reaction to Monger's
pronouncement was skeptical. "My God," he

129

said, "if we got a CAG that's a fighter jock and we can't find MiGs, we sure aren't going to do it with a bomber jock."[5]

But Monger had a plan. He knew that historically fighters were best employed as wide-ranging, freelance hunters. Over Europe in World War II, General Jimmy Doolittle had released his Eighth Air Force fighters from flying close escort to the heavy bombers so that they could chase down the Luftwaffe interceptors before they could mass for attacks. But that was another time and another war. Monger noted that A-1 and A-4 pilots saw bandits when no one in VF-211 or its sister squadron, VF-24, had so much as a whiff of a MiG.

The reason was peculiar to the Vietnam War. The Communists had too few interceptors to deal with American fighters. If the NVAF was to make its presence felt, it would have to concentrate on the strike aircraft—as the two MiG-17s had done against the F-105s near Thanh Hoa. Related Commander Marr, "Jack Monger said that instead of spreading out our fighters in classic style, we'd stuff them right up with the strike group."[6] In short, if the F-8s couldn't get to the MiGs, *Hancock* fighter pilots would let the MiGs come to them.

Marr flew six missions in the first five days on the line, hoping Monger's idea would work. Nothing unusual happened. Then, on 12 June, "we were knee-deep in MiGs."[7]

Marr led a mini-Alpha off "Hanna" at noon. His wingman was Lieutenant (j.g.) Phillip Vampatella, with two VF-24 pilots as the second section. The four F-8Es escorted Skyhawks of VA-212 and -216 to a barracks complex north of Haiphong, dodging in and out of bad weather. Flying at 1,500 feet, the carrier pilots weaved around 3,000- to 4,000-foot mountains rising into a 2,000-foot overcast.

The target area was clear, however, and the

The first two F-8 pilots to shoot down MiGs were Commander H. L. Marr (right) and Lieutenant (j.g.) Phil Vampatella (left) of VF-211. Marr, the squadron commander, got his MiG on 12 June 1966. Vampatella shot down another MiG-17 nine days later. (U. S. Navy)

131

A-4s unloaded their bombs, getting good hits on numerous buildings. The strike came off the target, Crusaders tucked in behind the bombers, and headed north through a small mountain pass beneath a 3,500-foot broken overcast. As the formation turned starboard onto a northeast heading 30 miles out of Haiphong, Phil Vampatella called, "Tally ho. Bogies at seven o'clock."

Marr looked back under his port stabilator and saw four smoke trails, about a mile and a half back at 2,000 feet. They were MiG-17s, pushing hard in afterburner to overtake the Americans. Marr and Vampatella broke hard left and down, pulling heavy Gs to turn into the threat. Simultaneously the MiGs split, two banking tightly to stay with Marr, the other pair heading towards Lieutenant Commander F. D. Richardson's VF-24 section.

This was what Hal Marr had been waiting for since he won his wings back in 1948. He had logged nearly 4,000 hours in props, jets, and helicopters, including 1,500 in Crusaders. And now he was exactly where he wanted to be—entering a duel with enemy fighters.

The two F-8s and two -17s met almost head-on through their turns, straining at 450 to 500 knots and pulling five to seven Gs. Marr snapped out a hopeful burst of 20-mm at one MiG, but it was "for courage more than anything else."[8] Reversing hard to starboard, the Checkmate skipper pulled his nose through another MiG passing 500 feet ahead at wide angle, fired again, and missed again.

Scissoring on the bandits once more, the two F-8s were gaining an advantage. Marr and Vampatella had maneuvered to the MiGs' seven o'clock, forcing them to split the section. Each Crusader pursued its respective opponent. Marr followed his MiG in a left-hand turn, watching it bob up and down. He fired another optimistic burst of 20-mm, but he was out of range.

The CO was now in command of the situation, however. The MiG had boxed itself into a small valley under the low clouds. At a distance of roughly 2,500 feet, Marr was out of gun range so he selected "Heat" on his armament switch. Closing on the MiG's port quarter about 1,000 feet above, he fired his first Sidewinder. But the angle was too wide, and the missile fell to earth.

By now the -17 pilot decided to call it quits. Marr estimated that the MiG had been in afterburner at least four minutes, and saw it roll out of its turn and head for home, undoubtedly running out of fuel. It was too good an opportunity to pass up. He rolled level, lit his burner, and gave chase at 500 knots indicated. With the range down to half a mile he launched his second 'winder, which "zapped him real fine."[9] The missile chopped off the tail and starboard wing, sending the MiG tumbling end over end into a small hamlet on the bank of a river.

Emerging from below the clouds, Marr found two more -17s in a medium-banked left turn. Hardly able to believe his good fortune, he turned in behind the MiGs at 200 yards, drew a bead, and opened fire with his cannon. But the guns abruptly quit after a few rounds—an electrical failure stopped them cold. Marr's aim was good, however, and he saw large pieces fly off his target's starboard wing. But the -17 had a dry wing—no internal fuel tanks—and the last Marr saw, the MiG was floundering for home.

Hal Marr decided on the same course of action. He selected afterburner and made 600 knots into the clouds, to avoid visual tracking by AA guns. He was the last pilot back over the boat, conscious that he'd knocked down the fourteenth MiG of the war, and the first ever by a Crusader. The occasion called for something special, so Marr radioed the air boss and announced (rather than requested) a celebratory fly-by. It was contrary to standard procedure,

133

for victorious pilots had been known to have their airplanes fall apart in their laps executing victory rolls, due to undetected battle damage. But as far as anyone knew, the -17s hadn't fired a round. And besides, how often does an aviator bag his first MiG?

Marr screamed down the portside of the "Hanna," making about 600 mph, so low that he looked up and saw the deck-edge elevator above him. Then he honked up in a wide barrel roll, turned back into the pattern, and dirtied up the airplane. Speed brakes out, gear down, wing up. Settling into the groove, Marr hit the angled deck—and boltered off the far end. In his exuberance he'd forgotten to extend his hook.

Next time around he trapped safely into "the wildest reception the world's ever seen."[10] The *Hancock*'s skipper, Captain Jim Donaldson, announced that from then on, any pilot who bagged a MiG could make a no-hook pass and the captain would cheerfully pay the customary five-dollar fine into the party fund. Amid the noise and riotous hubbub of the celebration, Marr learned that Phil Vampatella had worked his way to the second MiG's tail but inflicted no damage. The other two -17s also escaped at low level.

But the jinx was broken. The Crusader had drawn first blood, and more opportunities were forthcoming. Nine days later Vampatella got his wish for another chance, but under different circumstances than he would have desired.

On 21 June, four *Hancock* Crusaders were called in to provide CAP for a downed recon pilot until a rescue helicopter arrived. The photo bird had been hit by flak near Hanoi, and the pilot ejected into a valley well inland. To compound matters, the weather remained soupy with a 3,500-foot overcast and reduced visibility.

The ResCAP F-8s orbited by sections in the valley, planning to rotate on station by alternating
quick trips out to waiting KA-3 tankers offshore.

The Crusaders were fired upon regularly
during their orbits, and Vampatella took a hit
somewhere aft. But his instruments showed normal readings, and the twenty-six-year-old New
Yorker chose to remain. After about twenty minutes in the area, Vampatella followed his section
leader towards the coast, low on fuel. But shortly
they heard the division lead call, "Tally ho!
MiGs!"[11] The other F-8s were only about 10
miles astern, so Vampatella's section immediately reversed course. It was then that Vampatella realized his plane was badly damaged. He
couldn't keep pace with his leader, and by the
time he got turned around he was thirty seconds
behind.

Entering the fight, the two reinforcements
evened up the odds at four all. Vampatella
turned towards a MiG-17, then looked up to
starboard and saw a bandit behind an F-8, in
range and gunning. He hollered a warning for
all Crusaders to break right, not knowing who
was in the vulnerable F-8, but it was too late.
Even as he turned to help, the Crusader's tail
exploded and Lieutenant Cole Black punched
out. He spent six and a half years in Hanoi.

Enraged and frustrated, Vampatella
checked his own six o'clock and found another
MiG closing. He went to afterburner and
wracked his Echo into a shuddering, diving turn,
temporarily breaking the -17's tracking. But the
bandit stayed with him, and at 2,500 feet, still in
burner, Vampatella pulled a desperation maneuver. He rolled inverted and sucked the stick
back. He recovered from his frantic Split-S right
on the trees, hoping the MiG wouldn't make it,
and came out of burner to conserve fuel. The
-17 was still there, but Vampatella had gained

135

some distance. He stayed right down on the deck, jinking and weaving, in and out of burner, barely in control.

At 600 knots, his aircraft slewing about all three axes, his helmet bouncing off the canopy, Vampatella reluctantly disengaged afterburner. "I had to slow down or die," he recalled.[12] But when he looked back to check the MiG, he saw it had given up and turned away.

At this moment, Phil Vampatella was presented with a devilish dilemma. He was over enemy territory in a damaged airplane, rapidly running out of fuel. In fact, he was now beyond "bingo" fuel and couldn't get all the way back to the ship. The best he could hope for was a fast rendezvous with a tanker. He thought of his two shipmates on the ground, of the MiG flying leisurely home, and of his pregnant wife back in the states. "But in the final analysis," he said, "there was really no choice at all."[13]

Vampatella's blood was up and he opted for revenge. He reversed course, checked his armament switches again, and closed on the unsuspecting bandit. He centered the swept-wing MiG in his sight, heard the tone in his earphones which told him his 'winder was tracking, and pressed the button. The AIM-9 came off the rail, wavered momentarily, then enabled and smoked toward the hot tailpipe ahead of it. Vampatella selected another Sidewinder just in case, but the first one did the job. It exploded and dropped the MiG into a burning, headlong dive.

Phil Vampatella barely registered the elation of his kill when his attention was drawn to the fuel gauges. Heading outbound, uncertain whether he could even make the shoreline, he hollered for any available tankers to meet him over the beach. He was feet wet on the deck at 550 knots with an estimated eight minutes flying time remaining. Fortunately, he was followed on

U.S. radar and received a steer to the nearest KA-3.

The crippled F-8 popped up to 20,000 feet where Vampatella spotted the Skywarrior, decelerated and closed in. His tanks contained about five minutes worth of flying time. But the Crusader was feeling the effects of its damage, and became unstable at refueling airspeed. Vampatella was not sure he could plug in before he flamed out, though there was one big source of comfort below. He spotted a "gorgeous sight, the destroyer *Coontz..*"[14] If the worst happened, at least he could eject with excellent prospects of rescue.

After repeated attempts, Vampatella inserted his refueling probe in the basket and began to receive JP-4. But his troubles weren't over. This particular tanker had topped off several other planes, and could only give him 700 pounds. The way it looked, he'd probably make the 60 miles to the *Hancock*, but if he didn't get aboard on the first pass he'd most likely get his feet wet. Therefore, Vampatella called ahead, requesting maximum wind over the deck, immediate clearance for a straight-in approach with no waveoff, and a helo airborne astern the ship.

Escorted by another VF-211 pilot who described the visible damage, Vampatella made straight for the *Hancock*. There was no time to experiment with controllability in landing configuration, so he hoped for the best—and got aboard on his first try. Maintenance personnel counted over seventy small shrapnel holes from the one hit by a 37-mm explosive shell.

Vampatella's safe return wasn't the only good news of the day. Lieutenant Eugene J. Chancy, the -211 division leader, also knocked down a -17. He fired a Sidewinder but destroyed the MiG with guns. In ten days the Checkmates

137

had dumped three MiGs, losing one F-8, and Commander Monger was proven as good as his word.

Following this series of defeats, the MiGs seemed to switch tactics. With the carriers launching three Alphas a day, the Communist interceptors preferred to contest the last strike, since late afternoon gave them the additional advantage of sun and reduced visibility. To counter this new development, the *Oriskany's* air wing shifted its formation. The CO of VF-162 was stocky, aggressive Commander Richard M. Bellinger, who wanted to put the TarCAP flight well ahead of the bombers. He hoped the enemy radar would interpret this as an unescorted bomber division, and vector MiGs to it.

It was a calculated risk, with obvious dangers, but Dick Bellinger was willing to gamble. He had a wealth of experience to draw upon, as he'd been in air corps bombers during World War II. He returned to college, enrolled in navy ROTC, and became a naval aviator in 1950. "Belly" had flown Banshees in Korea and qualified in Crusaders during 1957.

The new strike formation was tried for the first time on 17 July. One of the Hunters' F-8Es got a downcheck before launch, so Bellinger proceeded with two wingmen under a 2,500-foot solid overcast. And sure enough, the bandits took the bait. Five MiG-17s bounced the three Crusaders, and for the next few minutes a low-level rat race ensued, with two MiGs ganging up on Lieutenant (j.g.) Chuck Tinker, Bellinger's number two (who'd suffered radio failure), while the CO and his number three, Lieutenant Dick Wyman, tried for a shot at another -17. Turning hard at 350 knots, with sustained loads of five or more Gs, some pilots flew so low they had to pull up to avoid trees and buildings. Wyman's guns jammed under heavy G loads, and he pickled a Sidewinder, which homed on some ground object.

Bellinger had just pitched up to 2,000 feet, preparing to yo-yo back into the fight and cut off the third MiG's turn, when the missing pair showed up. They hauled into gun range and clobbered Bellinger's Echo. His right stabilator was completely gone with most of the right outer wing panel, his fuel tanks were holed, and hydraulic pressure dropped. The stricken F-8 rolled wildly, and as Bellinger fought for control the MiGs ceased fire. It looked as if they'd scored a kill.

But Bellinger regained control, reduced power, and headed out of the fight at about 225 knots, using the low clouds for concealment. Once over the coast he turned south for Da Nang, knowing he'd never get aboard in his present condition. He'd have made Da Nang if his refueling probe hadn't been damaged, but he flamed out forty miles short and safely ejected. Back aboard the *Oriskany* the next day, the Hunter skipper vowed next time it would be different.

And it was. Three months later, on 9 October, Air Wing 16 provided strike escort for the *Intrepid*. Bellinger again had things carefully arranged. He obtained the services of an E-1B early-warning aircraft and had it positioned offshore as an airborne radar station. The Tracer could warn the strike escort of approaching MiGs while Bellinger's flight orbited low in mountainous terrain near the target. Thus hidden under the enemy radar screen, VF-162 hoped to surprise any MiGs sent to engage the bombers.

Like all passive weapons systems, whether ECM or early-warning aircraft, the E-1s were among the least-publicized carrier aircraft of the war. But they had a share in the activity this time, and Bellinger's local Tracer made possible what followed. Alerted to MiGs approaching from the northwest, 90 miles out, Bellinger's pilots monitored the E-1 reports. When the Tracer's radar showed definite bandits 40 miles from the target, the Hunters departed their mountain hiding place.

Nearing the target only 300 feet over the ground, Bellinger searched high and forward, knowing that was where the MiGs would appear. And he was right. The MiGs—they were -21s—sped into view at about 3,000 feet. It was obvious they were unaware of the low-flying F-8s.

Bellinger had set his trap carefully, and now he sprang it. He lit the burner, boomed toward the bandits, and slid into firing position directly behind the two nearest targets. Bellinger selected the enemy wingman and was ready to shoot when the intended victim belatedly saw the threat. The -21 could maneuver well at high speed, and the MiG driver did a split-S, knowing the F-8 on his tail couldn't complete the same maneuver at low level.

But Bellinger had his teeth into this MiG, and refused to let go. He followed the -21 into its half-roll and began his pull-through. As the Crusader's nose came through the horizon, with both fighters diving vertically, Bellinger fired two Sidewinders. Frequently the missiles malfunctioned in such instances, as the ground could present a better heat source than the target aircraft's tailpipe. So Bellinger wasn't wasting a shot by firing twice. It was sound doctrine, as it doubled the probability of a hit.

Playing the percentages did the trick. The first 'winder homed to the target and blew off one wing. The second, close behind, detonated from its proximity fuze. Bellinger had a glimpse of the -21 falling in flames, but was instantly occupied with more pressing matters. He was headed almost straight down at high speed, very near the ground, without much hope of pulling through to complete the split-S. Even if he avoided impact, the terrible G-load would probably induce structural failure.

Immediately Bellinger slapped the stick to one side, abruptly centering it to complete a half-roll. Now, with a slightly better angle relative to the rice paddies looming in his windscreen, he pulled as hard as he dared. His G-suit constricted and the airframe protested under the abnormal aerodynamic load. But the Crusader came level at perhaps 200 feet—not much over the trees—pulling streamers from the wingtips. Bellinger shot a fast glance at the wreckage of the MiG on the ground, and though other bandits remained in the area, he did not pursue. They were no immediate threat, and the F-8s shepherded the bombers back out to sea.

Bellinger's was the first MiG-21 knocked down by a navy pilot, and only the fourth of the war. Ten months would pass before the carrier fliers bagged another delta-winged MiG, and seven months until the next F-8 kill. But it was a familiar team that returned to the job.

In January of 1967, Air Wing 21 sailed to the Tonkin Gulf for its third Vietnam cruise. Now embarked in the *Bon Homme Richard*, VF-24 and -211 intended to resume Air Wing 21's record as the navy's biggest distributor of MiG parts. Not until May did things warm up again, but when it did the Checkertails and Checkmates enjoyed the best hunting of any navy fighter jocks in the first half of the war. This cruise would net the "Bonny Dick" Crusaders eight MiGs.

On 1 May, the traditional Communist holiday, Commander Marshall O. Wright of 211 tangled with a -17 and killed it with a Sidewinder. That same day an Air Wing 21 Skyhawk pilot, Lieutenant Commander Ted Schwartz, bagged another -17 in the pattern at Kep with a load of

*An ebullient Commander Dick
Bellinger describes his MiG-21
kill upon return to* Oriskany *in
October 1966. (Drendel)*

Zunis. Nearly three weeks later 211's CO led a mixed 24 and 211 division into the biggest hassle any navy pilots had seen up to that time.

Commander Paul Speer, formerly Hal Marr's exec, took a strike to Hanoi's thermal power plant on 19 May, the first trip "downtown" for the air wing. "Bonny Dick's" Skyhawks had the new Walleye glide bomb, a deadly accurate 1,000-pound weapon aimed by TV camera. The Skyhawks of VA-212 had initiated the Walleye to combat against the Thanh Hoa Bridge in March, and three glide-bombs had struck within a six-foot circle. In combat the Walleye achieved a fantastic record, with 95 percent hits. It wasn't enough to topple the Dragon's Jaw, but it would take out most other targets.

"Bonnie Dick's" strike involved two A-4Es of VA-212 escorted by a dozen Crusaders, F-8

Charlies and Echoes, of VF-24 and -211. Each Skyhawk packed a Walleye intended for the power-generating building. Half of Speer's Crusaders carried four Sidewinders apiece, while the others packed six Zunis for flak suppression and one 'winder.

Inbound to the target, opposition increased tremendously. Lieutenant Commander Bobby Lee of VF-24's flak-suppression flight recalled the AAA as "worse than I have ever seen." And of course the SAMs were active, too. The pilots counted over thirty missiles fired their way.[15]

Paul Speer's division was flying TarCAP, protecting the A-4s from possible interception, when one of those odd combat events occurred. Out of nowhere, blithely ignorant of the situation, a MiG-17 flew through the formation. Speer's wingman was Lieutenant (j.g.) Joe Shea, whose comment became legendary in Crusader circles. "There's a MiG among us," intoned Shea. "No one get excited. . . ."[16]

Perhaps nobody got excited, but they became exceedingly eager. Lieutenant Phil Wood, an Oklahoma pilot in VF-24, was detached to run off the MiG, which he did. He rejoined formation, flew through all calibers of flak, then was bounced by another MiG that hit his plane with gunfire. But Wood outfought the offending -17 and killed it with a Sidewinder.

Meanwhile, the flak-suppression F-8s continued with the bombers. Bobby Lee and his wingman located their assigned antiaircraft site and fired their Zunis into the battery. But the SAMs remained troublesome, and in the fury and confusion it wasn't possible to see all of them. Two Crusaders were hit, and both pilots ejected. As they descended in their chutes toward the enemy's heartland, they knew there was no hope of rescue. Both were captured and spent five and one half years as POWs.

By now the A-4s had dropped their Walleyes

143

and the strike headed outbound. But more MiGs were drawn to the area, and the Americans estimated perhaps a dozen bandits in the vicinity—some now mixed in with the carrier planes. It was obvious the Crusaders would have to shoot their way out.

And that's what they did. Paul Speer and Joe Shea each tagged on to a -17, and both pilots scored confirmed kills with 'winders. For a moment in the confusion it wasn't certain who had done what to whom. Speer called Shea, asking, "I saw yours, did you see mine?" Back aboard ship, the CO took more than a little ribbing from his troops. "Imagine," said one 211 pilot, "pulling rank on your wingman just for a kill! It was all good-natured, though."[17]

But it wasn't over yet. Another MiG-17, evidently no more alert than the first one, flew alongside the flak-suppression flight and slowly curved in front. Bobby Lee could hardly believe his good fortune. This turkey was meat on the table. Lee had been a naval aviator for nine years, logging 2,500 hours total time and about 1,600 in Crusaders. However, most of that was in RF-8s, and this was his first combat cruise.

One of the biggest dogfights in the F-8's career occurred on 19 May 1967 when Air Wing 21 Crusaders escorted strike aircraft to Hanoi. MiGs intercepted, and four were shot down by Hancock *pilots, including one each by Commander Paul Speer (left) and Lieutenant (j.g.) Joe Shea, both of VF-211. (U. S. Navy)*

144

The Floridian turned hard behind the un-wary MiG at 700 feet altitude and selected the "Heat" station on his armament switch. With just one Sidewinder, he wanted the best shot he could get. Closing the range, pulling several Gs, Lee decided it was now or never. He fired and felt the missile come off the airplane. Immediately he wished he could call the 'winder back. It looked as if he was too close to the target, and the AIM-9 headed well outside the turn.

Lee thought, "Damn, it's the only missile I have."[18] He was just accepting the disappoint-ment when the Sidewinder got a whiff of the heat source and turned back in front of the F-8, tracking for the MiG's tailpipe. The proximity fuze detonated a few feet from the -17's fuselage and cut the bandit in two immediately aft of the wings. Lee watched the MiG's severed tail rotate to the outside of the turn while the front half fell to earth from under 700 feet. There was no time for the enemy pilot to eject.

Still heading west, the Crusaders made for the mountains just south of Hanoi that separate Laos from North Vietnam. It was a circuitous route home, but the safest way. And just as the formation steadied on course for the coast, a silver MiG-17 came alongside, out of control. "He crashed below us and rolled through the fields in a huge fireball," Lee said. It was prob-ably one of the victims of VF-211, but which one was not determined.[19]

In this engagement, the *Bon Homme Richard* Crusaders had bagged four of the sixteen MiGs sent against them, raising Air Wing 21's wartime tally to nine. Counting the -17 destroyed by a VA-76 Skyhawk on 1 May, it amounted to six kills on this tour alone, in less than three weeks. Down in 211's readyroom, somebody noticed that Paul Speer, Moe Wright, and Joe Shea all had aisle seats, and they had the first three kills of the 1967 cruise. That fourth seat would have

145

auctioned for a thousand dollars if the CO had allowed it.

The hassle of 19 May took the wind out of the MiGs' sails for eight weeks. There were only scattered sightings by navy pilots in that time, but no combats. However, when the bandits came up to fight again, they were met by the same team, as eight Crusaders from VF-24 and -211 were riding shotgun once more.

It was a strike escort against the fuel depot at Ta Xa, 25 miles northeast of Hanoi on 21 July. The large Alpha strike involved some two dozen attack aircraft, while Lieutenant Commander Marion H. Isaacks led a four-plane TarCAP. Red Isaacks, who hailed from Redding, California, was the new Checkertail exec, with only two or three flights "over the beach" in VF-24. But he was an experienced aviator, confident in the F-8 as "last of the single-seat fun birds."[20]

Isaacks' division was flying at about 10,000 feet, slightly ahead of the strike group, when he saw three or four silver MiG-17s pop up out of the clouds. There were others in the area, too, and the odds stacked up to an even fight with eight MiGs and eight Crusaders.

Isaacks transmitted "bandits" on the strike frequency, picked a MiG, and went after it in a climbing port turn. The exec moved to the hostile's six o'clock and fired a Sidewinder. But the missile failed to track. Well, no matter; Isaacks had three more and he was still in the saddle. He pressed the trigger again, anticipating the familiar lurch when a 'winder left the rail, but it never came. His second missile failed completely.

Now Isaacks was worried. He was down to two Sidewinders and the fight had hardly begun. But he maintained a firing position, and pickled his third AIM-9. And it was third-time lucky. The 'winder smoked out, tracking perfectly, and

went straight up the MiG's tailpipe. There was a bright scarlet fireball in the sky, and Isaacks watched, fascinated. This was what it was all about—the endless training, the separation from family, the dreary chores and unpleasant assignments. It all came together right here.

And it was just such thoughts that could get a fighter pilot killed. Isaacks' reverie was abruptly shattered when tracer shells flashed past his starboard wing. "I glanced down to my right and found myself looking down the intake of another MiG," he recalled.[21]

Reacting instinctively, the XO hauled his Crusader into a diving right-hand turn to meet the threat head-on. At a relative closing speed of over 850 knots, the two fighters were nose-to-nose when the MiG pilot half-snapped to inverted and sucked the stick into his stomach. The -17's evasive split-S came barely in time, for Isaacks was rocked by the displaced air of the MiG's passage.

Only then did Isaacks realize that the MiG had scored. Some 23-mm shells had punctured the hydraulic control lines in the starboard wing

A VF-24 F-8H snags a wire during Hancock's *1969 deployment, still bearing the four MiG-17 silhouettes symbolic of victories during the 1967 cruise in* Bon Homme Richard *(CVA 31). (Peter B. Mersky)*

147

Crusader hit by AAA east of Hanoi 26 October 1967. The pilot was Lieutenant Chuck Rice, who became a POW.

near the aileron, starting a small fire. Turning east, Isaacks squawked Mayday over the emergency channel and headed for "Bonnie Dick." He preferred to risk an inflight explosion rather than eject over North Vietnam.

The punctured controls continued to feed hydraulic fluid to the fire, and for a long, long forty-five minutes the wing continued to burn. When the fluid finally ran out, the fire died and Isaacks was left to ponder the backup system. If the pneumatic secondary controls were undamaged, he had a good chance of getting aboard. Over the boat, Isaacks raised his wing, lowered hook and wheels, and crunched down in a safe trap after an eventful two and a half hours.

The exec found that his other pilots had also been fully occupied. Lieutenant Commander Bob Kirkwood, a Massachusetts Checkertail pilot, made Crusader history by shooting down a MiG-17 exclusively with his guns. When the bandits pounced, Kirkwood turned in to engage and fired his first Sidewinder, causing the MiGs to confront the F-8s. Kirkwood's next 'winder was fired at another -17, but a few seconds late. He saw Red Isaacks' missile take the MiG apart before his own arrived.

Determined to get a kill, Kirkwood engaged a third MiG-17, maneuvered into good firing position, and launched his last 'winder. The AIM-9 tracked well, but exploded alongside without inflicting visible damage. The Vietnamese turned right, and Kirkwood followed, charging his guns. He squeezed the trigger at 200 yards and continued firing, closing the range. The 20-mm shells sparkled over the MiG's wings and fuselage, followed by a gush of flame. Kirkwood saw the -17 pitch up, the canopy came off, and the pilot ejected as the F-8 passed close by. Like Isaacks, Kirkwood returned with battle damage. En route home he learned that three-

148

quarters of his starboard stabilator was gone, but he got down safely.

Fighting 211 also hung a MiG scalp on its lodgepole. Lieutenant Commander Ray Hubbard, the colorful Checkmate LSO, used every means at his disposal to kill his victim. Assigned to flak suppression, "Tim" Hubbard had only one Sidewinder, which he fired unsuccessfully at the nearest MiG. He followed up the missile attack with gunfire, scoring hits while narrowing the range. Then two more -17s crossed his nose and Hubbard turned to follow.

Without a Sidewinder, and out of gun range, Hubbard salvoed four Zunis at the MiG wingman, still turning. It looked as if one rocket hit, and the bandit rolled wings level, allowing the Crusader to narrow the gap. Hubbard fired the last of his 20-mm load into the -17, and it was enough. The MiG driver punched out, almost hitting the F-8E.

The seven-minute combat of 21 July resulted in three confirmed kills and a probable against two damaged F-8s. The uncertain claim was that of Lieutenant (j.g.) Phil Dempewolf of 211, who clobbered a -17 with a Sidewinder. But just as Dempewolf fired, two MiGs had threatened his section, and his missile shot wasn't followed.

This scrap raised Air Wing 21's wartime total to twelve kills—by far the greatest number in the navy at that time. Eleven were credited to the Checkertail and Checkmate F-8s, while VA-76's kill made it an even dozen. No other air wing would kill as many MiGs through the rest of the war.

Not all MiG encounters resulted in kills—not half. But sometimes just getting home was satisfaction enough. That is basically the difference in attitude between fighter pilots of World War II and those of Vietnam. The World War

II jocks speak of victories. The 'Nam vets speak of survival.

One such pilot was Lieutenant Commander R. W. Schaffert, a thirty-three-year-old professional with 3,500 hours of fighter time, who found he needed every bit of his experience and training to stay alive.

Fighting 111 was VF-162's sister squadron aboard the *Oriskany* for the 1967–68 deployment, and the Sundowners on this cruise may have been the most experienced group of Crusader talent ever assembled. The pilots averaged over 1,200 hours in type, led by Commander Bob Rasmussen, a former Blue Angel.

Dick Schaffert was assigned to escort an A-4E flown by Lieutenant (j.g.) Chuck Nelson on 14 December 1967. They comprised the second anti-SAM section for a strike of six Skyhawks, while Commander Cal Swanson and Lieutenant Dick Wyman of VF-162 provided

Fighter Squadron 111, USS Oriskany, Tonkin Gulf, November 1967. Back row (left to right) Commander Bob Rasmussen (CO), Lieutenant (j.g.) Jake Jacobsen, Lieutenant (j.g.) Craig Taylor, Lieutenant Commander Dave Baker, Lieutenant (j.g.) Tom Garrett, Lieutenant Commander Pete Peters, Lieutenant (j.g.) Carl Stattin, Commander Jack Tinney (XO). Front row (left to right) Lieutenant Commander Dick Schaffert, Lieutenant Al Astin, Lieutenant Commander Bob Jenkins, Lieutenant (j.g.) John Laughter, Lieutenant Jay Meadows, Lieutenant (j.g.) John Sande, Captain (USAF) Andy Anderson.

TarCAP. The A-4s were to mine the "Canal of Bamboo" between Hanoi and Haiphong, so enemy reaction was expected to be stiff. And it was.

Schaffert's F-8C was armed with three AIM-9Ds, as the fourth had failed its flight deck inspection. But he also packed 400 rounds of 20-mm at launch about 1600 hours. Nearing the coast, monitoring strike frequency, he heard a warning, "Two red bandits airborne at Bullseye."[22] That meant MiG-17s taking off from Gia Lam airfield. Their progress was monitored by offshore radar ships—Red Crown and Harbor Master—and as the strike went feet-dry, the reports indicated that the interceptors were headed due east. Schaffert charged his guns, switched on his Sidewinder coolant, and energized his ECM gear.

Attracted by hostile radar emissions to the south, Chuck Nelson turned port and led Schaffert that way, intending to loft a Shrike at the tracking site. Meanwhile, the MiGs were nearing the strike group in a head-on intercept as the A-4s rolled in to attack. Then Harbor Master called Swanson on TarCAP, warning him of hostiles three miles west of him. That made no sense to Schaffert. The MiGs shouldn't have been able to close the strike group, which was now turned outbound.

Nelson's A-4E was then climbing to the southwest amid the warbling indications of a SAM launch. Schaffert figured Nelson was about to fire a Shrike, and watched from starboard at 18,000 feet. Just then he noticed a reflection below the sun, at eleven o'clock low. There were two MiG-17s, less than a mile away.

Schaffert keyed his mike. "Pouncer Three, we got two MiGs passing below us to the left."[23] Then he broke hard down to gain airspeed, but refrained from afterburner to reduce the chance of being spotted. If he played it just right, and

Lieutenant Commander R. W. Schaffert of VF-111, who fought four MiG-17s in an F-8C on 14 December 1967 and lived to tell the tale. (Schaffert)

151

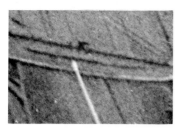

MiG-17 over Thai Binh 14 December 1967. Sidewinder fired by Commander Bob Rasmussen, CO, VF-111. (Schaffert)

Commander Rasmussen's Sidewinder misses. (Schaffert)

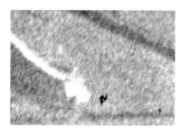

MiG-17 kill over Thai Binh 14 December 1967. The MiG broke to avoid Sidewinder fired by Commander Bob Rasmussen of VF-111 (trail across photo). Another Sidewinder, fired by Lieutenant Dick Wyman of VF-162, scores direct hit and MiG explodes. (Schaffert)

had some luck, he could bag one or two MiGs. But the -17s saw him coming, punched off their drop tanks, and turned into him. Chuck Nelson called, saying he saw the MiGs but had lost Schaffert. Just then the F-8 bottomed out of its yo-yo, in burner, climbing back toward the bandits 3,000 feet above and still turning in.

Schaffert glanced over his shoulder to look for Nelson and got the fright of his life. Two more -17s in close-fighting wing formation had pounced out of the sun, tracking him for a gunnery pass. They were only 3,000 feet out, and Schaffert was sure he was about to get clobbered. At 450 knots indicated, pulling up through the horizon, he snapped the stick over, loaded about eight Gs on the Crusader, and pulled hard. With the F-8 shuddering on the ragged edge of a stall, the MiGs slid outside the radius of his turn without firing.

Now began a ten-minute exercise in survival. Opposed by four MiG-17s, without a wingman, Dick Schaffert knew he was in "deep serious." He hollered to Bob Rasmussen, still with the strike group, to come help. But his high-G break forced his oxygen mask down over his chin and he was unable to use his radio for the remainder of the engagement. He was on his own.

When the two newcomers overshot, Schaffert went over the top of his high yo-yo and came back down almost vertically on the first pair of -17s. Well-positioned at the leader's six, about 3,700 feet back, he had a good Sidewinder tone. But the steep nose-down attitude gave the missile an excellent view of the water in the rice paddies, and he withheld the shot. Pulling his nose up for better deflection, Schaffert was about to continue his attack when tracers sparkled over his left shoulder. The second MiG section had quickly regained position. These boys were good! The leader was 2,500 feet out, and gunning. Schaffert noticed that the MiGs' three guns were all firing at a rapid, even rate, and it occurred to him that he was up against late-model -17s with three 23-mm guns. It meant his opponents might have afterburning engines as well.

Three more times Schaffert pulled hard reversals, then attacked the pair that presented the best opportunity for a shot. Returning to the first two, he heard the growl of his first 'winder and fired at about 20 degrees angle-off. The MiG leader saw the shot guiding toward him and turned extremely hard into the missile, which passed between the leader and his number two without exploding. It was a heartbreaker; the missile missed its target by less than 40 feet. Proximity fuzes failed several F-8 pilots about this time, and Schaffert's Sidewinder was also a dud.

Yo-yoing up to about 15,000 each time and diving back into the fight, the lone F-8 had to stay aggressive. If he tried to evade he'd be cold meat. At one point the two -17s on his tail both fired two Atolls from wide deflection at about 4,000 feet range. The angle was too extreme, and all four went wide. His own second shot failed to guide.

Schaffert then dropped down on the other section's wingman, who had drifted wide from his leader. With a clear background to the east, Schaffert fired his third and last 'winder from 20 to 30 degrees angle-off at about 3,000 feet. Not bothering to watch the missile, he followed the MiG leader in a left turn, pulling six Gs, closing for a gun shot.

With over 500 gunnery flights behind him, Schaffert was confident he could hit anything in range. He was tracking well at 30 degrees deflection, closing at perhaps 150 knots relative overtake. His gyro-stabilized gunsight was pegged at 1,500 feet, and at 1,000 feet he placed the pipper slightly ahead of the MiG. He in-

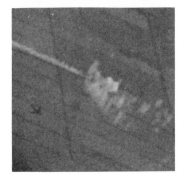

A low-level chase over the rice paddies near Thai Binh on 14 December 1967 is shown in this sequence. Several Sidewinders were fired by Oriskany *pilots before Lieutenant Dick Wyman made the kill. Commander Cal Swanson, VF-162 skipper, said of the MiG pilot: "He was a tiger. He came to fight." (Peter B. Mersky)*

153

tended to fire one burst, pulling his sights through the target. Dick Schaffert now owned the -17, if only his guns would function.

At 800 feet range, still at five to six Gs, he squeezed the trigger. One or two rounds, then silence. The high-G maneuvers had robbed him of air pressure to the pneumatic feeder system. Then the tracers came from behind again; the troublesome first MiG was 1,000 feet behind.

"I suddenly felt very despondent with all my firepower gone, and in a definitely defensive situation," Schaffert recalled.[24] It was a masterful understatement. But help was on the way. Bob Rasmussen was coming at full steam after seeing the A-4s safely over the beach. And Chuck Nelson, bless his soul, was following one of the -17s in his Skyhawk, coaching the skipper to the fight.

Meanwhile, Schaffert threw a high-G roll under the attacking MiGs, and they pulled up, finishing about 2,000 feet above him. Schaffert then honked his F-8 Charlie upward in a vertical rolling scissors. After the third evolution, the enemy wingman was thrown out of the hassle and did not rejoin. Schaffert and the MiG leader continued their vertical duel. At about the fifth scissors the two fighters were canopy to canopy. The -17's superior turning radius was telling, and Schaffert felt himself gradually losing position.

Over the top the sixth time his altimeter showed 5,000 feet. Time to get out. Schaffert stuffed his nose down, pushed his throttle through the detent into afterburner, and held his vertical plunge as long as he dared. A mind-blurring high-G pullout was accomplished less than 100 feet above the ground. Making 500 knots indicated, Schaffert noted a red fuel warning light. He had 1,350 pounds remaining. That decided it. He noted the MiG a mile back, apparently not closing, came out of burner, and began a slow climb. Flying right down the Red

River, with 15 miles to the coast, he finally saw the -17 turn west.

Schaffert called Cal Swanson, telling him the MiG's position, but by now the VF-162 section had joined Chuck Nelson and Bob Rasmussen. Three Crusaders now pounced on the lone MiG that Nelson had been trailing in his A-4, and several Sidewinders were expended to no effect. Like Schaffert, the pilots experienced maddening proximity-fuze failures.

Finally the 70-mile rat race bottomed out at rice paddy level. Swanson's wingman, twenty-eight-year-old Dick Wyman, got a good opportunity and launched an AIM-9D, which took off the -17's port wing. The MiG splashed from 50 feet up.

Schaffert flew a maximum-range profile for the 113 miles to the *Oriskany* and, unable to join a tanker, made a straight-in approach. He caught the wire with less than 200 pounds of fuel. "My only solace was when Dick and Cal almost ran into each other doing their victory roll over the ship," he concluded.[25]

Dick Schaffert had barely survived on the short end of four-to-one odds. "I needed every ounce of experience I had to come away from that mission intact," he said.[26] Had he not known his aircraft so well from 1,500 hours in type, he might not have succeeded with his treetop pull-out. Low-level hassling was seldom condoned in training, as it was considered too dangerous. But Schaffert and others admitted to a lot of flat-hatting. Now and then it saved lives.

At the end of 1967, navy pilots had shot down twenty-eight North Vietnamese aircraft. Twelve were credited to Phantoms (including two propeller-driven AN-2s), while A-1 Skyraiders had bagged two MiG-17s and an A-4 dropped one. The remaining thirteen were done in by three Crusader squadrons: VF-211, -24, and -162. The Checkmates were top guns

A flight-deck crewman runs from under an F-8 Crusader seconds before launch from the USS Hancock (CVA 19) to intercept a Russian "Bear." The Soviet aircraft was observed in the vicinity while the ship was in the Western Pacific in early August 1968. (U.S. Navy)

with seven kills, while the most successful F-4 squadron was VF-114 off the *Kitty Hawk*, claiming two MiGs and an AN-2.

Aerial combat was greatly reduced during the first half of 1968. Air force Phantoms bagged eight MiGs during January and February, and a VF-96 F-4J claimed a MiG-21 kill in May. Then, on 26 June, VF-51 drew blood for the first time in Vietnam.

Three "Screaming Eagle" F-8Hs were over the Tonkin Gulf following an escort when they were informed of bandits near Vinh Son, 150 miles south of Hanoi. The Crusaders had just come off a tanker and, flush with fuel, headed inland at "Buster" speed.

Lieutenant Bert Harden, a twenty-five-year-old Texan, saw the MiGs first. As the Crusaders made a hard turn over Vinh Son, Harden looked up and saw a pair of -21s at two o'clock high. He called the tally-ho, and the formation leader, Commander Lowell R. Myers, also picked them up. Apparently the enemy pilots saw the F-8s at the same time, as they released their fuel tanks. The opposing fighters headed toward each other, the MiGs above and the Crusaders from below.

At thirty-five, Moose Myers was ten years older than his two wingmen. But he had 181 missions behind him, and he'd seen MiGs before. He was confident in himself and his aircraft, and when the lead MiG overshot, Myers knew he had him.

When the -21 passed overhead, Myers was already bending his Crusader through a hard turn that put him astern the bandit, climbing at about 45 degrees. It was an excellent firing position, and Myers launched a single Sidewinder. The missile homed on the exposed tailpipe, and exploded there. Myers saw the empennage was "completely gone" with flames trailing from both wing roots as the shattered MiG went down.

Myers' second wingman, Lieutenant John Quisenberry, watched the -21 roll and seem to reverse, as if returning to the fight. Quisenberry pulled up, preparing to shoot, but then noticed the MiG was afire as the seat came out. He was close enough to see that the pilot wore a black flight suit. The second MiG sped north, and the VF-51 trio watched Myers' victim as it "just kind of floated down and crashed in a ball of flames."[27] The wreckage hit the ground about 45 seconds after the combat began.

Like other successful engagements, this one was the result of lengthy training. A naval aviator for twelve years, Myers had 2,900 hours in Crusaders and was well prepared for air combat. He called the MiG kill "the biggest thrill of my life," and estimated he'd practiced it "a thousand times if I've practiced it once."[28]

Still, the effect wasn't felt until Myers led his flight back to the *Bon Homme Richard*. As he reported his intention to land aboard, the LSO

157

replied, "Roger MiG killer." Said Myers, "It felt great."[29]

Two weeks later another high-time Crusader pilot bagged a MiG in the same area. On 9 July, the *Ticonderoga* launched a photo-recce section to cover the region north and south of Vinh, a few miles inshore in Route Pack III. Lieutenant Commander John B. Nichols III from VF-191 was assigned to escort an RF-8 of VFP-63 flown by Lieutenant William Kocar. Nichols described Kocar as "one of the very best F-8 pilots, and his expertise was very useful even though he was unarmed."[30]

Nichols himself was no novice. With approximately 2,800 F-8 hours in his logbook, he had flown all versions of the Crusader, including the French model. He had spent four years in VF-62 and three years instructing in VF-174. During 153 missions he had experienced three MiG encounters.

On this sortie, Nichols flew an F-8E with single pylons (meaning two AIM-9Ds), plus a full load of 20-mm belted in armor-piercing, fragmentation, and tracer. The Echo was Nichols's favorite of the Crusader line, and he was pleased to find that all his systems were up. His armament switches were set for Sidewinder firing on the button, and guns on the trigger of his stick grip. His radar, he found, "worked perfectly for a change, even in the gun ranging mode including audio signals."[31]

The section coasted in north of Vinh, continued to Vinh Son where Kocar took several photos, then turned south and followed the Song Ca River to Vinh. The sky was perfectly clear with 22-mile visibility, and the two Crusaders were fired upon all the way. Kocar was flying too low for Nichols's comfort, about 2,000 feet above ground level, so Nichols was spread wide to starboard in "loose deuce" at about 5,000 feet.

They approached Vinh from the west, indicating 475 knots.

Then Nichols saw a green MiG-17 approaching the RF-8 from port, two miles back and closing fast. Nichols transmitted a hurried warning, instructing Kocar to break left. Without pausing to look, the photo pilot made a hard-nose down turn, pulling over six Gs. Nichols also broke hard to port, straining through a 90-degree bank at about five and a half Gs.

Halfway through his turn, Nichols had a good Sidewinder tone, telling him his first missile was tracking as he continued to roll nosedown. The quick photo response had thrown the -17 to the outside, and Nichols was lining up for a shot. Tracers flashed past from an unseen second MiG, but Nichols coolly ignored them and pressed his attack.

Still in a wrapped-up turn, Nichols fired his right-hand missile. "It guided and appeared to have a chance of scoring, but the Gs were apparently too much," he said. "The Sidewinder passed well outside the right-hand side of the MiG and exploded harmlessly."[32]

But the 'winder wasn't wasted. Apparently confused by the explosion, the MiG pilot reversed his left-hand turn and rolled to the right. Nichols was now dead astern, at zero G, about 1,200 feet back, beautifully positioned to kill. To make matters worse for himself, the MiG driver foolishly selected afterburner, which removed any doubt the port Sidewinder may have had about its target.

The -9D went directly to the -17's tailpipe, where it exploded. "The sky in front of me was full of small pieces of metal," Nichols said, "and the MiG began to leave a trail of what I believe was fuel."[33] But surprisingly, the MiG continued its right-hand turn, intact, though decelerating rapidly. Fearful of overshooting, Nichols

Commander John Nichols, CO of VF-24 in 1972, scored the F-8's fifteenth aerial victory while flying with VF-191 from Ticonderoga (CVA 14) in July 1968. He finished his career as one of the five high-time Crusader pilots with more than 3,000 hours in type. (Peter B. Mersky)

brought his throttle back to idle power and popped full-speed brakes to stay in the saddle. He was riding the MiG's tail 300 feet back, and settled his gunsight on the front of the target at slight deflection.

Nichols's finger depressed the trigger for what he thought was a short burst. He was surprised to learn back aboard ship that he had fired 160 rounds. But it mattered little. He observed several hits, and the MiG disintegrated. Nichols rolled abruptly to port to miss some of the larger pieces. The wreckage hit the ground nose-first, about 60 seconds after Nichols first spotted the bandit.

Kocar had remained in position to cover Nichols's tail during the hassle, even though the photo bird couldn't fight. Still hungry, Nichols turned starboard, accelerating to fighting speed, and looked for the second MiG. But there was no sign, and though Kocar wanted to hunt for it, Nichols decided to call it a day. He was out of Sidewinders, running low on 20-mm, and had under 4,500 pounds of fuel remaining. Feet-wet south of Vinh, the Crusaders hit the tanker and recovered aboard the *Ticonderoga* without damage.

In the postmortem, Nichols attributed the MiG's demise as much to its pilot's stupidity as to the F-8's assets. In allowing himself to get sandwiched between two enemy aircraft, and compounding that error by reversing his turn, the MiG driver sealed his own fate. Post-mission photos showed the dead Vietnamese still in the debris of his aircraft. Intelligence officers told Nichols the enemy pilot was twenty-three years old with 450 hours total time. "He flew like it," Nichols concluded.[34]

Through the summer and fall of 1968, Crusaders were bagging MiGs at the regular interval of one a month. The *Bon Homme Richard*, long the top MiG-killing carrier, continued its string while operating Air Wing 5 in July and August. On 29 July Lieutenant Commander Guy Cane, VF-53's exec, downed a MiG-17 in what he likened to "a classic World War I dogfight."[35]

Cane's wingman, Lieutenant (j.g.) Dexter Manlove, sighted the bandit first. The -17 was high and right, silhouetted against a cloud. Manlove called the tally-ho, then spotted two approaching head-on. As usual, it developed into an even contest, with four planes on each side.

Cane maneuvered into a firing position and loosed a Sidewinder. "It detonated just short of his tailpipe," Cane related. "I thought I had missed until a chunk of his starboard wing came off and the MiG went into a nose dive, spiralling."[36]

Three days later, the first of August, VF-51 and -53 double-teamed a MiG-21. Lieutenant George Hise of VF-53 noticed "this dartlike form" in his peripheral vision. The -21 fired an Atoll that went wide. "I knew we were fat then," explained Lieutenant Norman McCoy, "because the MiG turned to the right and we were both in a position to chase him."[37]

With the MiG caught between two hungry Crusaders, Hise fired a 'winder that damaged the bandit. Then McCoy launched a missile that exploded immediately next to the target's fuselage, at the wingroot. Streaming flames, the -21 dropped in a near vertical dive. It hit in a mountain range, erupting in a large fireball. It was the eleventh kill by a "Bonny Dick" Crusader.

Rounding out the "MiG-a-month" ratio was VF-111 in September. The Sundowners had a small detachment aboard the *Intrepid* with the all-attack Air Wing 10. Though 111 was on its third Vietnam cruise, it had not yet scored a MiG kill. However, the squadron had lost a plane to MiG-17s in September 1966, with the pilot becoming a POW.

The Sundowners traced their ancestry directly to VF-11 of World War II fame, with a redesignation in 1948. Flying Wildcats and Hellcats from 1943 to 1945, Fighting 11 had 158 "meatballs" on its scoreboard by V-J Day, plus a MiG-15 for good measure in Korea. Then, on 19 September 1968, the Sundowners recorded the 160th shootdown of their long career.

Two F-8Cs were launched from the *Intrepid* on an intercept. Lieutenant Anthony J. Nargi, the section leader, spotted a bogie and closed for visual identification He eyeballed it as a MiG-21, which attempted to evade in a loop. Nargi followed, closing the distance.

Now within the Sidewinder's lethal range, Nargi fired. It was a perfect launch as the missile guided directly to the target's tailpipe and exploded. The MiG's tail separated from the fuselage in a red fireball, and the pilot ejected. Nargi saw the orange and white parachute deploy, but was then attracted to another bandit. His wingman, Lieutenant (j.g.) Alexander Rucker, had spotted a second MiG, and both Crusaders fired Sidewinders. The two missiles detonated close to the Communist fighter, but it escaped northward.

Back aboard ship, Tony Nargi speculated upon the significance of his lucky number. His MiG kill came while flying his 111th mission with VF-111 from CV-11. No crapshooter could hope for better odds.

Nargi's was the last MiG ever shot down by an F-8. In the twenty-seven months since Hal Marr's victory, eighteen Crusader pilots had scored confirmed kills. They represented seven squadrons flying from five carriers, though the *Bon Homme Richard* was way out in front of the pack. "Bonny Dick's" Crusaders bagged eleven

MiGs as the aggregate total of VF-24 and -221 with four apiece, plus VF-51's pair, and VF-53's single. Next was the *Hancock* with three shoot-downs, all by 211. Fighting 162 bagged a -17 and a -21 aboard the *Oriskany*, while the *Intrepid* and *Ticonderoga* F-8s each splashed one MiG.

Nearly two-thirds of the F-8 victories were made by Echoes, reflecting that model's wide use in Vietnam. Charlies accounted for five kills, while two MiGs fell to F-8Hs. But the Crusader clan's record as a whole was quite impressive. During 1968, navy aircraft shot down six MiGs, of which five were felled by Crusaders. And for the period 1965 to 1968 inclusive—that portion of the war prior to the bombing halt—F-8s dominated the carriers' air combat statistics. In those three years, carrier air wings recorded thirty-four MiG kills. Phantoms claimed thirteen while A-1s and A-4s splashed three more. The Crusader's eighteen victories represented about 53 percent of the navy total at the time.

From the fall of 1968 to the beginning of 1972, aerial combat almost ceased to exist in Southeast Asia. The only MiG shot down in that three-year interval was a -21 splashed by a VF-142 Phantom in March of 1970. The air force, without benefit of operating offshore where the rules of engagement still allowed occasional encounters, scored no kills from February 1968 to February 1972.

No pursuit was authorized into North Vietnamese airspace owing to the political atmosphere in Washington and Paris, where "peace talks" continued. But navy pilots sometimes saw MiGs that ventured into international waters. An experience that would be maddening to any fighter pilot occurred during the *Ticonderoga*'s 1969 WestPac deployment. Lieutenant Tom Weinel of VF-162 was airborne on ForceCap when the Red Crown controller, whom he knew, asked Weinel to switch to the secure voice channel. Weinel, an Annapolis grad with a tomcat smile and a cavalier attitude, met the controller on the designated frequency.

"You should have been here a little while ago," said the FDO. "We had two MiGs out here and they both got away."[38] Weinel groaned inside his oxygen mask. Two F-4s had contacted the bandits and closed to about a mile dead astern. But neither Phantom pilot realized they were authorized to shoot on sight outside the three-mile limit. By the time the task force commander roared his approval, saying no authorization was necessary, the MiGs were back over the beach.

Weinel did get one chance at a MiG. While flying another CAP, his division was alerted to at least one bogie heading toward the task force. The fighter director, unable to keep the excitement out of his voice, vectored the F-8Js due west at "Buster" speed. That meant full bore. The Juliets leapt forward as afterburners kicked in and the pilots "turned on every damned switch in the cockpit."[39] With pulses pounding and a silent supplication to the gods of war for *just this one chance*, the Crusaders raced westward at over 700 knots.

The range was down to 20 miles and the MiG was still coming. At 15 miles the pilots were staring holes in the sky trying to catch a glimpse. Then, at 14 miles, the controller came on again. The lone bandit had turned back toward shore, no longer a potential threat. Tom Weinel remembers it as the longest return flight he ever made.

North Vietnamese aircraft weren't the only bogies that caused some excitement, however. The Red Chinese airfields on Hainan in the Tonkin Gulf sometimes put up pesky investigators. On occasion, MiG-19s paced navy aircraft back towards their ships—an unsettling experience, since regulations required that a potential adversary initiate hostile action before a U.S. pilot could shoot in self-defense. At least one F-8 pilot confessed that if any Chinaman had tried to tail *him* back home, "I'd have murdered the SOB and learned to live with it." A pilot could easily claim the MiG turned towards him, thereby posing a threat, but air discipline held. Not cheerfully, but it held.

The air war slowly increased tempo in early 1972. Lieutenant Randy Cunningham, an F-4J pilot off the *Constellation*, bagged a -21 in January—the first of his five kills. The Sundowners of VF-111, now flying F-4Bs, dropped a -17 in March. Then in May, with more restrictions lifted as the Nixon administration finally tired of three years of fruitless negotiating in Paris, the war entered its final phase in the North. Haiphong harbor was mined, air strikes resumed in force, and the MiGs came up once more to fight. Phantom crews licked their chops in anticipation. Crusader pilots muttered dark oaths; they weren't getting any shooting.

Nevertheless, the last F-8 victory was obtained that way: without shooting. On 22 April, Lieutenant Commander Frank Bachman and Lieutenant Jerry Tucker of VF-211 launched from the *Hancock* as TarCAP for an Alpha. The Checkmates were back on the job aboard "Hanna," just where Hal Marr had started things six years before. The two F-8Js orbited offshore while the strike birds hit their targets in the hourglass area of the delta.

The Alpha was already feet-wet when bandits were reported on the guard channel. Bachman and Tucker switched to Red Crown's frequency and offered their services. The controller replied that two VF-161 "Rock Rivers" were going after a lone MiG headed south. Still orbiting off the beach, the 211 pilots listened with growing frustration as the F-4s lost sight of one another and attempted to rendezvous over hostile territory.

At this point, Jerry Tucker "had heard all I could stand."[40] The F-8s told Red Crown they were intact and available to take a vector, so the FDO cleared the Crusaders inbound while ordering the *Midway* Phantoms out.

Bachman and Tucker were feet-dry between Nam Dinh and Nin Binh, heading for the MiG's last known position. After a search of the area, which yielded nothing, they began taking ground fire and decided to exit. Heading east, Tucker caught a glint, low to the north. "I padlocked the speck," he said, and informed Bachman.[41] The section turned to port, heading north, and Tucker distinguished a MiG-17 down near the treetops. It was heading south at high speed. If not for that momentary gleam off the canopy, Tucker never would have seen it.

Frank Bachman still didn't have the bandit, so he wisely turned over the lead to his wingman. Tucker pitched up to port to roll in behind the -17 for a Sidewinder shot. Roughly a half-mile behind the MiG, Tucker saw the bandit abruptly drop its nose. Almost simultaneously, a white parachute blossomed in the sky and the MiG exploded on the ground. The MiG driver apparently had seen his peril at the last moment and scuttled rather than fight.

Tucker made two passes around the chute— the most intriguing sight he'd seen in the 800 hours he'd spent in F-8s. But instead of an enemy pilot dressed in black, Jerry Tucker saw his Silver Star dangling under that big white canopy. While the MiG hadn't technically been shot down, depriving Tucker of his medal, a hostile had been destroyed. The Red Baron study credited him with a kill—the only one attributed to a Juliet.

During the course of the war, American aircraft shot down 198 MiGs (and 2 prop-driven aircraft), for the known loss of 76 planes in air combat. Of the air-to-air losses, 66 were fighters, for an overall kill-loss ratio of 2.6 to 1, and a fighter exchange rate of 2.8 to 1. Phantoms claimed nearly 75 percent of all shootdowns.

The Navy's ACM record was tagged at 5.8 to 1, largely due to carrier-based Phantoms that bagged some thirty-seven MiGs for the loss of six in air combat. But the war's best kill record was run up by the Crusader, with only three losses to MiGs against nineteen victories—an exchange rate of 6.3 to 1. Yet the total U.S. exchange ratio early in the war was barely two and one half for one. How to explain the difference?

As previously mentioned, hassling had gone out of style in the late 1950s and early 1960s. Fighter pilots trained with more emphasis on interception, strike, and ground support than in plain old-fashioned red-dogging. Missiles were the thing. There was little use in practicing dogfighting if you were going to blow your opponent out of the sky from several miles away. Of course, it didn't work that way in Vietnam. Only after the 1968 bombing halt did the navy evaluate its combat lessons and establish the Fighter Weapons School at NAS Miramar. "Topgun" graduates knocked down twenty-four MiGs for two losses when the war brewed up again in 1972, but by then the Crusaders's best days were past. In 1972–73 they mainly flew ForceCAPS, BarCAPS, recons, and photo escorts.

Therefore, insufficient training for the ACM role was probably the main reason for both navy and air force pilots' disappointing early record. They simply weren't prepared to hang in a six-G turn at 5,000 feet, trying to remain in the Sidewinder's performance envelope. There were exceptions, of course, but they were found in units whose leaders recognized the difference between theory and reality.

Vietnam's tactical environment also affected

167

the U.S. success ratio. Political restrictions, particularly in the first two and a half years, placed American aircrews at a significant disadvantage. The insane edicts from Washington regarding sanctuaries and rules of engagement actually favored the enemy. The Johnson administration in particular seemed more concerned with protecting Russians than Americans. This, combined with much unimaginative, unprofessional planning, target selection, and routing, worked to the benefit of the MiGs more than once. That Crusaders were knocking down MiGs at six for one when other aircraft were barely breaking even is all the more remarkable, for everyone flew in the same circumstances.

None of the foregoing should be interpreted as a denigration of the other aircraft—particularly the Phantom. There were F-8 pilots who openly admired the F-4, and some who contended (at their own peril!) that the Phantom was a better aircraft. But it was true. No other airplane in the world performed so wide a variety of jobs so uniformly well. In this respect, the F-4 was a pentathlon winner while the F-8 was a champion hurdler. Weighing 60 percent more than the Crusader, the Phantom possessed a greater payload capacity, somewhat more speed, and a good deal more "stretch." But it was never the fighter pilot's fighter plane that the Vought was from the beginning.

This, then, is what the Crusader community meant when it coined its oft-quoted boast, "When you're out of F-8s, you're out of fighters."

The Crusader Goes International

7

Following Vietnam, the Crusader's decline seemed certain. But the Vought had a grasp on the future that was easily traced to the prewar era. And the future was not limited to the United States, for the Crusader had gone cosmopolitan.

The route to international acceptance was indirect. It began with the seventy-seventh production F8U-1.[1] Bureau Number 143710 was converted to a two-seat trainer by installing a second cockpit immediately aft of the original. The rear seat was raised fifteen inches above the front in order to improve visibility, but full controls were installed.

Designated the F8U-1T by the navy (and "Twosader" unofficially by Vought), the one-of-a-kind fighter first flew on 6 February 1962. As usual, John Konrad was behind the stick. Two of the 20-mm cannon were removed to make room for the extra cockpit, but otherwise the trainer was equipped like the new F-8E, with four Sidewinder rails. Top speed was within 0.05 Mach of single-seat F-8s.

Anticipating new operating environments and the possibility of full production for the two-seater, Vought experimented with rough field capabilities. The Twosader was equipped with a

169

drag chute and low-pressure tires that allowed it to land in 2,700 feet, which was barely half the distance it took a conventional Crusader.

Later that year, when the military aircraft designation system was standardized, the two-seater became the TF-8A. Vought had eyed European markets for the Crusader, and the new model flew to Paris for the annual international airshow. For two weeks at the British aeronautical engineering establishment at Boscombe Down, nearly thirty RAF and Royal Navy pilots took turns flying the "one-off" Vought. Older RAF and Fleet Air Arm jets, such as the Hawker Hunter and DeHavilland Sea Vixen, were approaching obsolescence, and Vought hoped a two-seat Crusader would fill the gap. Certainly it had the potential. As a fighter and strike aircraft, it could perform both land- and carrier-based missions. And the second seat afforded excellent prospects for supersonic training in contemporary front-line aircraft.

Another argument in favor of the TF-8A was cost. At the time, F-8Es rolled off the line with government-furnished equipment for under one million dollars a copy. That was £ 340,000, not counting the saving in design and engineering costs. The Rolls-Royce Spey engine producing 20,000 pounds thrust was considered for British F-8s, which with boundary layer control would provide better performance and about 20 percent more range. But the Royal Navy opted instead for the two-million-dollar Phantoms, and F-4Ks were among the last carrier aircraft flown by the Fleet Air Arm.

Meanwhile, the U.S. Navy still hoped to obtain more TF-8As. But the Fiscal 1964 budget request, which included some additional two-seaters, was denied. After the Twosader's job was done at Vought, it went to the Naval Air Test Center at Patuxent River, Maryland, for additional test and evaluation. From there the lone TF model was lent to the National Aeronautics and Space Administration.

In 1977 Vought received a contract to overhaul 25 F-8Hs for the Philippine Air Force. The PAF would have preferred F-15s or F-16s, but regarded the Crusader as the best buy for available funds. The Hotels had been in storage at Davis-Monthan AFB, Arizona, where the dry climate preserved them from climactic deterioration. Enough pickled aircraft were withdrawn from storage to meet the basic requirement of the PAF, and ten additional airframes were provided as a source of spare parts for ten years. It was an accurate estimate. By 1988 the Philippine Crusaders were grounded for lack of spares, with no replacement fighter being considered.

As part of the Philippine program, the TF-8A was recalled from NASA to assist in the transition training of Filipino pilots. Resplendent in its white and blue NASA color scheme, the Twosader set about introducing a new crop of airmen to the F-8. But the work was short-lived. On 28 July 1978 Vought pilot Ken Fox was up with Lieutenant Pascualito Ramos, south of Dallas. Fox experienced engine trouble and tried to reach an uncongested area for a possible forced landing. But it was too late, and both pilots were forced to eject. The Twosader crashed in a peanut field, ending more than sixteen years of service to the navy, Vought, NASA, and Britain.

The one and only F8U-1T, redesignated TF-8A in 1962. (Vought)

One of twenty-five F-8Hs supplied to the Philippine Air Force in 1978–79. (Vought)

Fox and Ramos returned safely to Dallas via company helicopter.

The failure of the two-seater to reach production, however, was in large part overshadowed by another foreign contract. When the Philippine Air Force received reconditioned F-8Hs in 1978, the French Navy had been flying its own F-8Es for about fourteen years.

One of the potential selling points for European Crusaders was the F-8's adaptability to smaller carriers. And since France produced the only new strike carriers in the world outside the U.S. and Britain after WW II, the Aéronavale was a logical customer. The 22,000-ton *Clemenceau* was commissioned in 1961, followed by her sister *Foch* in 1963, when France still was dependent upon Britain and America for most of her carrier aircraft.

Actually, the Aéronavale was no stranger to Vought products. Following the Second World War, Corsairs were widely used throughout the dwindling French empire. France's American-built light carriers operated F4U-7s and AU-1s in campaigns over Indochina, Algeria, and Suez before the bent-wing U-Birds were replaced by jets. But within two years of the *Foch*'s commissioning, Aéronavale's jets also were headed for retirement. Primarily these were DeHavilland Sea Venoms, called Acquilons by the French. The twin-boomed DH had been operational aboard carriers since 1954, when it became the Royal Navy's first all-weather jet fighter. But ten years later, its 575-mph (500-knot) top speed was inadequate by half. The French Navy again looked to Dallas.

The TF-8A's impressive performance at the Paris Airshow, combined with Vought's interest in expanded markets, focused attention on the Crusader. The *Clemenceau* and *Foch* were too small for navalized versions of most French aircraft, though the supersonic Dassault Étendard IV was successfully converted to a carrier strike fighter. But a vacancy remained in French naval aviation, and the F-8 seemed to fill the gap. It was small and light enough to fly from French carriers without much difficulty. The only major problem was the Crusader's minimum 113-knot landing speed, considered too hot for safe operation on board France's flattops, with their shorter catapults and smaller arresting gear.

Vought set to work reducing the F-8's takeoff and landing speeds. This involved sophisticated modifications to the entire wing, employing an extended droop of flaps, ailerons, and leading edges. The wing's camber was doubled with a 40-degree extension of flaps and ailerons, while the inboard leading edge droop was extended to 44 degrees and the outboard leading edge to 55 degrees.

Additionally, high-pressure bleed air from the J57 compressor section was forced over the ailerons and flaps through nozzles near the wing hinge line. This provided added lift without boundary layer control (BLC) separation. Thus, the variable incidence of the wing could be reduced from 7 to 5 degrees, with slightly enlarged stabilators to counteract the BLC's characteristic nose-down pitch.

This all amounted to a 9 percent reduction in the Crusader's stall speed, resulting in a landing speed of under 90 knots from the standard 113. An F-8D was fitted with the proposed French wing and was successfully test-flown in February 1964. The Delta crashed in mid-April, but the wing tests were completed by the first French F-8E beginning in late June.

The new bird was called the F-8E(FN), for French Navy, and the original order called for forty single-seaters and six TF-8s. The cost of the package would have run sixty million dollars, including 50 percent spare engines, but when Congress turned down the production Two-sader, France's desire for an F-8 trainer was quenched. Consequently, Aéronavale ordered forty-two fighters, a backlog of spare parts, and an electronic simulator. The last Crusader was an F-8E(FN) delivered in January 1965. The unit cost amounted to $1.4 million.[2]

The French Navy has kept the Crusader for what it was intended, "and never tried to turn it into a dumptruck," according to one flying admiral.[3] The FNs were optimized for aerial combat, retaining the four 20-mm cannon and the adaptability for Sidewinder missiles. But France already had an established armament industry, and the Matra R.530 mounted on fuselage rails was the primary air superiority weapon. Later, the Matra "Magic" R.550 was adopted—sometimes described as a Super Sidewinder. It is powered by a two-stage Hotchkiss-Brandt solid-propellant rocket motor that can drive the missile at Mach 2.7. This capacity, with a 60-pound warhead and an 11-mile range, explains the "magic" in the R.550.

Nevertheless, some early problems were experienced with the French missiles. The R.530

emitted searing flame at launch, and live tests showed skin damage to the F-8's fuselage and stabilators. For a while, Vought considered installing titanium stabilators, but a less-expensive fix was employed. Six-inch titanium leading edges were installed on the stabilators, and that solved the problem.

Aéronavale Crusaders conducted carrier qualifications with U.S. and French pilots aboard the USS *Shangri-La*, and were judged operational. The *Arromanches*, a French light carrier, shared ferrying duties with the *Foch* and took the F-8E(FN)s to the French naval base at Lann-Bihoue, where several were embarked in the *Clemenceau* for further trials in the Mediterranean during May 1965.

Once in the Med, a five-man team of French and American pilots began feeling out the FNs in their home environment. Launch and recovery tests showed that the Matra missile installation was secure for operations from French carriers, and the BLC system worked extremely well. Aboard the *Clemenceau*, pilots were making softer landings than possible in standard F-8Es, with a normal sink rate of eleven feet per second and an impact of under 3.5 Gs.[4] In fact, French pilots made ninety consecutive landings without a waveoff.

Anticipating joint operations later on, the pilots evaluated the compatibility of Franco-American equipment. The French F-8s already had flown from American carriers, and in the Med the *Saratoga*'s air wing provided U.S. Crusaders for reciprocal experiments. Commander Frederick Turner, "Sara's" CAG, made about twenty catapult shots and traps in a conventional Echo aboard the *Clemenceau* at different operating weights.

Flotilles 12F and 14F, the same units that had flown F4U-7s, had the original squadron assignments. Veteran French Navy pilots recall

175

that the Corsair's sophisticated systems had helped Aéronavale transition to jets with a minimum of difficulty. And the French continued their excellent record with Vought fighters. At first, twelve Crusaders were delivered to each squadron, but eventually 14F was re-equipped with Super Étendards. Therefore, 12F at Landivisiau became the primary F-8 unit.

Though Aéronavale seldom operated its Crusaders from carriers at night, its safety record was exceptional. In 1978, thirteen years after first delivery, the French Navy still was flying thirty-six of its forty-two Crusaders. More recently the F-8E(FN)s have been active from the *Clemenceau* in the North Arabian Sea, exercising regularly with F-14A Tomcats from American carriers. Flown with professionalism and elan, the remaining FNs will remain operational into the 1990s.

At least one other foreign marketing attempt was made, this time in the volatile Middle East. Two Crusaders were demonstrated to the Kuwaiti Air Force in May 1973, with an offer of 30 H and K models at $175,000 each, unrefurbished. The fighters were expected to be made available from storage in six months, but the offer languished and was not revived.

The Crusader's retirement as a U.S. Navy fighter came in 1976, after nineteen years of squadron service. And appropriately, the F-8 entered retirement in company with its longtime companion, the *Essex*-class carrier. True, Crusaders would fly for many more years as photo birds, and the tireless *Lexington* remained as the training carrier, but both now were fully replaced in their original roles in U.S. service.

The last deployment of a 27-Charlie was the *Oriskany*'s final WestPac cruise, which began in September 1975. She embarked Air Wing 19, the first and last all-Vought air group. Besides VF-191 and -194, a photo detachment of VFP-

The French Navy was still flying F-8E(FN)s in 1989, 25 years after receiving its first Crusaders. At that time they were expected to be replaced by F/A-18s until the French-built Rafale becomes available. (Peter B. Mersky)

63 rounded out the Crusader contingent. There were also three A-7 squadrons with the F-8's look-alike Corsair II attack planes. "Mighty O" returned home in March 1979, and "the last gunfighter" had hung up its guns.

Marine Corps Crusaders already had disappeared from the regular force structure. VMF-334 traded in its F-8Es for F-4Js in 1969, though at least nine navy and eight marine reserve squadrons flew F-8s at bases from Miramar to Dallas to Andrews. But most of the fighters were retired by 1976, when VMF-351 at NAS Atlanta became the last marine reserve unit operating the type. Its F-8Hs went into storage at Davis-Monthan with most of the other surviving Crusaders.

Consider the record of the last F-8J to pass through Miramar en route to storage in the Arizona desert. Bureau Number 149215 pulled onto Runway 24-Left on 19 May 1976, piloted by Lieutenant Frank Meyers of VFP-63. When Meyers lit the burner, lifted off, and headed east, his Crusader ended fourteen years of service. It bore the faded, sometimes peeling paint of VF-211, which had turned it over to VFP-63 for final repairs before its farewell flight. The Checkmates, of course, had rung up a superb record in Vietnam, with the most MiG kills of any F-8 squadron. But all that was history as VF-211 had transitioned to F-14s in 1975.

Number 215 had been delivered in 1962, near the end of the Crusader production run. Originally the 82nd F8U-2NE, it was the 1,012th Crusader to roll off the Dallas assembly line. With the designation change later that year it became an F-8E. Then, following remanufacture in 1969, old 215 became a J-Bird. At the time of its delivery to Davis-Monthan, the for-

Maintenance personnel prepare a VFP-306 RF-8G for an engine change. The scoops on the tail cone indicate this aircraft has undergone an engine modification, using the P-420 engine, originally used by fighter F-8s. The new engine gave a 33 percent power increase. (Peter B. Mersky)

mer *Hancock* fighter had logged 3,707 hours of flight time—85 percent greater than its original life expectancy.

By 1980 the RF-8G was the primary Crusader variant still on active duty. The largest unit was VFP-63, which continued supplying photo detachments to WestPac carriers in addition to maintaining "defanged" fighters for proficiency flying. In all, "Fightin' Photo" counted some thirty aircraft.

Among the reserves, three units at Andrews AFB near Washington, D.C., also flew photo birds. Two replacement air wings comprised the reserves' carrier component, and each had a "recce" squadron—VFP-206 in Air Wing 20 and VFP-306 in Air Wing 30. With a normal strength of four aircraft, the primary purpose of these units was to allow naval air reservists to maintain their flight time in fleet-type aircraft, should they be called to active duty.

Also at Andrews was VFP-6366, a squadron in the normal sense but minus aircraft. The pilots took turns flying the RF-8Gs of VFP-206 or -306, and when a vacancy occurred in one of those units, a replacement was chosen from 6366.

But even legends come to an end, and the Crusader saga began winding down during the early 1980s. VFP-63 was disestablished at Miramar 30 June 1982 after retrieving its last team—Detachment Two—from the *Coral Sea* and Air Wing 14.

During the decade, F-8s began disappearing from abroad as well. By the end of 1986 the Philippines' last twelve operational F-8Hs had been grounded for lack of support and spares. The PAF still flew Northrop F-5s, however, and began seeking buyers for its Voughts.

The F-4 and F-8 had their final sea period

"Cocooned" Crusaders at Davis-Monthan Air Force Base, Arizona, served as a source of spare parts for the dwindling supply of F-8s in U.S. and foreign service into the 1980s. (U.S. Navy)

together in U.S. Navy service when reserve squadrons VF-202 and VFP-206 logged their last catapult launches and arrested landings on board the *America* in October 1986. It seemed appropriate that the two fighters—longtime stable-mates and rivals—concluded their navy careers in concert. Five months later, VFP-206 rang down the final curtain in a gala, bittersweet event at Andrews AFB 28–30 March 1987. On hand was former Vought test pilot John Konrad, who watched Commander David Strong man up for the last U.S. Navy flight of a Crusader. An era had ended.

During its thirty-year career, the F-8 was flown by some 5,000 naval aviators, who logged 2,360,000 hours and 385,000 carrier landings. Five pilots recorded 3,000 hours in type, beginning with VF-191 CO R. A. Peters in 1971. He also set the record for most F-8 "traps" with almost 800 carrier landings. Fighting 24 commanders included David "Snake" Morris and John "Pirate" Nichols, both Checkertails commanders in 1972–73, followed by Jerry Unruh and W. F. "Bud" Flagg in 1974 and 1978. Flagg, Morris, and Unruh all became admirals.

Dedicated Crusader proponents such as these seldom were satisfied flying anything else, but the F-8 undeniably remained its own worst enemy. From start to finish, Crusaders recorded some forty-five major accidents per 100,000 flying hours. The F-14 averages fewer than ten major accidents per 100,000 hours.[5]

Nevertheless, with perverse pride former F-8 pilots actually boasted of their mount's dismal safety record. The aircraft's violent spin characteristics and delicate landing technique were cause for professional esteem as much as concern, and such traits were pointed out at the succession of "last annual Crusader balls" held at Miramar. The sixth of these was celebrated in May 1988, at which time it was noted that of 1,261 F-8s built, no fewer than 1,106 were involved in major accidents. There was a solemn moment, though, in which time was taken to honor the 186 pilots who died in Crusaders through the years.

Typical of the numerous F-8 zealots is re-

Photo aircraft of VFP-63 assigned to Carrier Air Wing 9 at NAS Miramar in 1979. The squadron, also known as "Fightin' Photo," was disestablished in 1982. (U.S. Navy)

The Naval Air Reserve was the last U.S. Navy user of the RF-8. Here two VFP-206 aircraft pose over the Potomac River with the Jefferson Memorial and the Washington Monument visible along the Tidal Basin in Washington, D.C. The last Reserve Crusaders were retired in 1986. (U.S. Navy)

A photo Crusader of VFP-206 taxis in from a mission during the winter of 1979. (Peter B. Mersky)

tired Commander Norm Gandia, an extroverted veteran of VF-33 and VF-174 "who thoroughly enjoyed some 1,300 hours in the pointy end of the Crusader."[6] Reflecting on his long association with the Vought, Gandia spoke for many enthusiastic fighter pilots when he said, "The Crusader was a beautiful machine, the highlight of my operational flying. Like a thoroughbred female, it required continuous attention, but the rewards were more than worth it. Flying the F-8, to quote an old friend of mine, was the most fun I've ever had with my clothes on. Its concept, design and utilization were so solid that it took almost ten years to screw it up with an air-to-ground mission and boundary layer control . . . F-8s forever!"[7]

In more subdued but equally heartfelt tones, similar sentiments were expressed by Commander John Nichols, a MiG-killer and high-time Crusader pilot: "I still believe that the F-8 was one of the world's great fighters, and the record of kills versus the MiGs should bear this out . . . To fly 'em was to love 'em."[8]

The Other Crusader

A

In 1955, early in the F8U-1 program, Russ Clark's engineers and aerodynamicists pondered the prospects of an even newer Vought fighter. The navy had not yet declared the need for a new VF design, but the signs were there for those who cared to hunt for them. Aviation ordnance was undergoing a revision, and mixed armament such as the F8U-1's seemed destined for obsolescence. Air-to-air missiles, particularly the radar-guided Sparrow family, were steadily gaining support over the guns.

The evolving concept was of a hard-climbing, high-flying, super-fast aircraft armed solely with long-range missiles. In short, an interceptor. Vought felt confident enough that BuAer would issue a requirement for such an aircraft that the design team set about reconfiguring the Crusader.

The Texans' optimism proved justified. In July 1955 the navy officially initiated its new interceptor competition, and the field was quickly narrowed to two contestants: Vought and McDonnell. The latter entry was a reworked version of a recent abortive attempt by the St. Louis clan to break into the attack business. The never-

184

to-be AH-1 thus emerged as the F4H-1, the "Phantastic Phantom," of which no further explanation is necessary.

Meanwhile, the updated Crusader similarly lacked much in common with its immediate ancestor. Though designated the F8U-3, some Vought personnel felt the new design should have been called the F9U-1. It was really an entirely new aircraft, with little more than a family resemblance to its namesake.

"Crusader III" was bigger and beefier than the F8U-1. With nearly five feet more wingspan and 30 percent greater wing area—not to mention over four feet more fuselage—the "dash three" was much larger than other Crusaders. And it weighed nearly two tons more, with a 20,000-pound empty weight in contrast to the F8U-1's 16,500.

Some F8U features remained, of course. Crusader III was a single-seater, though a two-seat configuration was considered in view of the navy's emerging preference. The variable-incidence wing was the most obvious similarity, but the differences were more notable: the stubbier vertical stabilizer, the forward-raked air intake, and the rotating ventral fins, for example. These were positioned below and forward of the stabilator and were locked horizontally in low-speed flight, but rotated downward for additional directional stability at high Mach. Boundary layer control was added, as were extended deflection of wing leading edges, flaps, and "drooperons." The new fighter's powerplant was the Pratt and Whitney J75, rated at about 25,000 pounds thrust with afterburner. Another difference was in the armament; it was limited to only three AIM-7 Sparrows.

In May 1957 BuAer gave Chance Vought the funds and approval for construction of two F8U-3s, and the number-one airframe was

185

nearly finished by New Year's Day 1958. Six months later John Konrad made the first flight, a 48-minute hop from Edwards Air Force Base.

Meanwhile, the navy had opted for sixteen Crusader IIIs, anticipating additional requirements for test, development, and operational research. Another change involved the "dash three's" weapons, expanded to include four Sidewinders. But the new Vought remained a missileer, first to last.

In the end, only five Crusader IIIs were built, and two of those never flew. The Phantom won the fly-off competition, largely due to its two-seat configuration and the presumed greater reliability of twin engines. The F8U-3 contract was canceled in December 1958.

Still, the Crusader III had much to commend it. Advanced avionics, allowing the pilot to fly and fight the aircraft by himself, were years ahead of anything else then flying. Automatic flight control was another feature. In fact, for a state-of-the-art aircraft, the F8U-3 experienced exceedingly few teething troubles. The test program involved only two noteworthy incidents. Test pilot Joe Angelone experienced a broken actuator on one ventral fin, locking the stabilizer in the down position. He had no choice but to land in that mode, and the fin was shorn off during landing at Edwards. John Konrad, certainly no stranger to trouble, had a compressor stall at about 75,000 feet but made a safe landing without power.

Every pilot who flew the III came away full of praise. John Konrad and Bob Rostine both considered it the finest aircraft they had ever flown. It was stable, rugged (designed for 6.5 Gs), responsive, and fast—very fast. The -3 was good for Mach 2.6 (1,750 mph at 35,000 feet), but its absolute speed was never attained. The windscreen glass showed signs of failure at near-maximum airspeed, and a tougher material

Though designated F8U-3, the Crusader III was in fact a wholly different aircraft from its predecessors: bigger and faster with Mach 3 potential. Large ventral fins for longitudinal stability at high altitude are folded while taxiing. The F8U-3 lost its contract bid to McDonnell's F4H-1 Phantom. (Vought)

could not be tested before the contract was canceled. Nevertheless, Chance Vought estimated the Crusader III was probably capable of Mach 2.9.

When the F4H won the fly-off, the "dash threes" went to NASA. Since the new Crusaders could fly above 95 percent of the earth's atmosphere, they were naturally useful for space research. They were also engaged in sonic-boom intensity studies, but more sporting diversions were occasionally found. The story is told that NASA pilots flying out of Langley, Virginia, gleefully bounced Phantoms undergoing evaluation at Patuxent River. The navy test pilots reportedly complained, and the sport ceased. But it had made Vought partisans feel a little better.

Eventually all F8U-3s were scrapped, and though some parts may remain, the ultimate Crusader has been outlived by its ancestors. But the III still survives in the minds of its designers and pilots as probably the greatest might-have-been in the history of fighter aviation.

Crusader Designations

B

Original Designation	Number Built	1962 Designation	Number Rebuilt	Rebuilt Designation
XF8U-1	2	XF-8A	0	No change
F8U-1	318	F-8A	0	No change
F8U-1E	130	F-8B	61	F-8L
F8U-1P	144	RF-8A	73	RF-8G
F8U-1T	(1)	TF-8A	0	No change
F8U-2	187	F-8C	87	F-8K
F8U-2N	152	F-8D	89	F-8H
F8U-2NE	286	F-8E	136	F-8J
F-8E(FN)	42	No change	0	No change
	1,261		446	

Specifications

C

F8U-1 **(F-8A)**	*Dimensions:* Wing span 35 feet, 8 inches. Length 54 feet, 3 inches. Height 15 feet, 9 inches. Same dimensions for remainder of the F8U series. *Engine:* Pratt and Whitney J57-P-4 and P-12; 10,000 pounds static thrust and 12,000 pounds in afterburner. *Armament:* Four Colt Mk12 20-mm cannon. Retractable rocket pack in speed brake with 32 2.75-inch rockets. Two AIM-9 Sidewinders on fuselage rails. AN/APG-30 fire-control system. *Remanufacture:* None.
F8U-1E **(F-8B)**	*Engine:* As F8U-1. *Armament:* As F8U-1, with AN/APS-67 radar, providing a limited all-weather capability. *Remanufacture:* Sixty-one aircraft rebuilt as F-8L with wing stations for external ordnance.
F8U-2 **(F-8C)**	*Engine:* Pratt and Whitney J57-P-16 with 500 pounds additional military thrust. *Armament:* As F8U-1 and -1E; capability of two additional Sidewinders. *Modifications:* Improved radar and fire control. Air intakes added to tailcone for increased afterburner cooling. Ventral fins added for improved directional stability. *Remanufacture:* Eighty-seven aircraft rebuilt as F-8K with A-7-type landing gear and strengthened wing.

189

F8U-2N   *Engine:* Pratt and Whitney J57-P-20; 10,700 pounds military
(F-8D)   thrust and 18,000 pounds in afterburner.
                Armament: Mighty Mouse rocket pack deleted.
                Modifications: AN/APQ-83 radar and AN/AAS-15 infrared scan-
                   ner gave this model a complete night-fighter capability. In-
                   creased fuel capacity and auto-throttle added.
                Remanufacture: Eighty-nine aircraft rebuilt as F-8H.
F8U-2NE   *Engine:* Pratt and Whitney J57-P-20.
(F-8E)   *Armament:* As F8U-2N.
                Modifications: Underwing pylons added, allowing up to 4,000
                   pounds of external ordnance. Larger nose cone to accom-
                   modate bigger AN/APQ-94 radar.
                Remanufacture: One hundred thirty-six aircraft rebuilt as F-8J
                   with boundary layer control, larger stabilator, double-droop
                   leading edges on wings, and capability of external fuel tanks.
F8U-1P   *Engine:* Pratt and Whitney J57-P-4A in F8U-1P and RF-8A. Pratt
(RF-8A)   and Whitney J57-P-22 in RF-8G.
                Armament: Five cameras in fuselage stations.
                Remanufacture: Seventy-three aircraft rebuilt as RF-8G, with four
                   camera stations and addition of ventral fins; additional navi-
                   gation equipment and electronics.
F-8E(FN)   *Engine:* Pratt and Whitney J57-P-20A with 700 pounds addi-
                   tional static thrust over the F-8E engine.
                Armament: As F-8E, with additional capability of Matra air-to-air
                   missiles.
                Modifications: As per F-8J.

Vietnam Cruises
by F-8 Squadrons

D

(Excludes photo detachments of VFP-62 and -63)

Air Wing 5

Apr–Dec	64	*Ticonderoga*	VF-51	F-8E	VF-53	F-8E
Sep 65–May	66	*Ticonderoga*	VF-51	F-8E	VF-53	F-8E
Jan–Jul	67	*Hancock*	VF-51	F-8E	VF-53	F-8E
Jan–Oct	68	*Bon Homme Richard*	VF-51	F-8H	VF-53	F-8E
Mar–Oct	69	*Bon Homme Richard*	VF-51	F-8J	VF-53	F-8J
Apr–Nov	70	*Bon Homme Richard*	VF-51	F-8J	VF-53	F-8J

Air Wing 8

Mar–Dec	70	*Shangri-La*	VF-111	F-8H	VF-162	F-8H

Air Wing 10

May–Dec	67	*Intrepid*	VF-111	(Detachment 11)	F-8C
Jun 68–Feb	69	*Intrepid*	VF-111	(Detachment 11)	F-8C

Air Wing 15

Dec 64–Nov	65	*Coral Sea*	VF-154	F-8D

Air Wing 16

Apr–Dec	65	*Oriskany*	VF-162	F-8E	VMF-212	F-8E
May–Nov	66	*Oriskany*	VF-162	F-8E	VF-111	F-8E
Jun 67–Jan	68	*Oriskany*	VF-162	F-8E	VF-111	F-8C
Feb–Sep	69	*Ticonderoga*	VF-162	F-8J	VF-111	F-8H

Air Wing 19

Jan–Nov	64	*Bon Homme Richard*	VF-191	F-8E	VF-194	F-8C
Apr 65–Jan	66	*Bon Homme Richard*	VF-191	F-8E	VF-194	F-8E
Oct 66–May	67	*Ticonderoga*	VF-191	F-8E	VF-194	F-8E
Dec 67–Aug	68	*Ticonderoga*	VF-191	F-8E	VF-194	F-8E
Apr–Nov	69	*Oriskany*	VF-191	F-8J	VF-194	F-8J
May–Dec	70	*Oriskany*	VF-191	F-8J	VF-194	F-8J
May–Dec	71	*Oriskany*	VF-191	F-8J	VF-194	F-8J
June 72–Mar	73	*Oriskany*	VF-191	F-8J	VF-194	F-8J

Air Wing 21

Oct 64–May	65	*Hancock*	VF-24	F-8C	VF-211	F-8E
Nov 65–Aug	66	*Hancock*	VF-24	F-8C	VF-211	F-8E
Jan–Aug	67	*Bon Homme Richard*	VF-24	F-8C	VF-211	F-8E
Jul 68–Mar	69	*Hancock*	VF-24	F-8H	VF-211	F-8H
Aug 69–Apr	70	*Hancock*	VF-24	F-8H	VF-211	F-8J
Oct 70–Jun	71	*Hancock*	VF-24	F-8J	VF-211	F-8J
Jan–Oct	72	*Hancock*	VF-24	F-8J	VF-211	F-8J

Crusader MiG Kills

E

Date	Pilot	Squadron (Ship)	Aircraft		Weapons
12 June 1966	Cdr. Harold L. Marr	VF-211 (19)	F-8E	MiG-17	Sidewinder
21 June 1966	Lt. Eugene J. Chancy	VF-211 (19)	F-8E	MiG-17	Guns
21 June 1966	Lt(j.g.) Phillip V. Vampatella	VF-211 (19)	F-8E	MiG-17	Sidewinder
9 October 1966	Cdr. Richard M. Bellinger	VF-162 (34)	F-8E	MiG-21	Sidewinder
1 May 1967	Cdr. Marshall O. Wright	VF-211 (31)	F-8E	MiG-17	Sidewinder
19 May 1967	Cdr. Paul H. Speer	VF-211 (31)	F-8E	MiG-17	Sidewinder
19 May 1967	Lt(j.g.) Joseph M. Shea	VF-211 (31)	F-8E	MiG-17	Sidewinder
19 May 1967	LCdr. Bobby C. Lee	VF-24 (31)	F-8C	MiG-17	Sidewinder
19 May 1967	Lt. Phillip R. Wood	VF-24 (31)	F-8C	MiG-17	Sidewinder
21 July 1967	LCdr. Marion H. Isaacks	VF-24 (31)	F-8C	MiG-17	Sidewinder
21 July 1967	LCdr. Robert L. Kirkwood	VF-24 (31)	F-8C	MiG-17	Guns
21 July 1967	LCdr. Ray G. Hubbard, Jr.	VF-211 (31)	F-8E	MiG-17	Zuni & Guns
14 December 1967	Lt. Richard E. Wyman	VF-162 (34)	F-8E	MiG-17	Sidewinder
26 June 1968	Cdr. Lowell R. Myers	VF-51 (31)	F-8H	MiG-21	Sidewinder
9 July 1968	LCdr. John B. Nichols III	VF-191 (14)	F-8E	MiG-17	S/W & Guns
29 July 1968	Cdr. Guy Cane	VF-53 (31)	F-8E	MiG-17	Sidewinder
1 August 1968	Lt. Norman K. McCoy, Jr.	VF-51 (31)	F-8H	MiG-21	Sidewinder
19 September 1968	Lt. Anthony J. Nargi	VF-111 (11)	F-8C	MiG-21	Sidewinder
22 April 1972	Lt. Gerald D. Tucker	VF-211 (19)	F-8J	MiG-17	None

Carrier			Squadron	Kills
CVA 11	Intrepid		VF-211	8 MiGs
CVA 14	Ticonderoga		VF-24	4 MiGs
CVA 19	Hancock		VF-51	2 MiGs
CVA 31	Bon Homme Richard		VF-162	2 MiGs
CVA 34	Oriskany		VF-53	1 MiG
			VF-111	1 MiG
			VF-191	1 MiG

Glossary

F

AAA	Anti-Aircraft Artillery.
ACM	Air Combat Maneuvering.
AIM	Air Intercept Missile, as in AIM-9 Sidewinder.
BarCAP	Barrier Combat Air Patrol: a standing patrol of fighters between a carrier task force and possible enemy attack.
Bandit	A hostile aircraft.
Bingo	A predetermined fuel state at which an aircraft must return to base.
BLC	Boundary Layer Control; ducting air over an aircraft wing in such a manner as to enhance low-speed lift and controllability.
Bogie	An unidentified aircraft, usually presumed hostile.
Bolter	Unsuccessful landing attempt, with failure of a plane's tail hook to engage the arresting wires. Usually in context of a carrier landing.
CAG	Literally, Commander of Air Group. A World War II term still used, though carrier air groups are now called air wings.

CAP   Combat Air Patrol.

CV   Standard abbreviation for an aircraft carrier. Occasionally also used to denote Chance Vought.

CVA   Attack carrier.

CVW   Carrier Air Wing.

Division A flight of four aircraft in most cases; two elements of two planes each.

DBR   Damaged Beyond Repair

DOD   Department of Defense.

ECM   Electronic Countermeasures.

FDO   Fighter Direction Officer.

ForceCAP Task Force Combat Air Patrol: a standing fighter patrol over or near a carrier task force.

GCI   Ground Controlled Intercept.

IR   Infrared, as in the heat-seeking capacity of the Sidewinder missile.

LSO   Landing Signal Officer.

LTV   Ling-Temco-Vought, formerly the corporate umbrella under which Vought Aircraft worked.

Mach   Properly, Mach's Number, after Austrian physicist Ernst Mach (1838–1916). The speed of sound, which varies with altitude and temperature. At sea level the speed of sound is nominally 762 mph, or Mach 1. Therefore, Mach 2 is 1,524 mph. But the figure diminishes with altitude, as Mach 1 at 10,000 feet is 735 mph, and is further reduced to 662 mph at 40,000 feet.

MAG   Marine Air Group.

MCAS   Marine Corps Air Station.

MiGCAP   MiG Combat Air Patrol: a roving section or division of fighters intended to engage MiGs attempting to intercept friendly aircraft.

195

NAA	National Aeronautics Association, the U.S. branch of the *Fédération Aéronautique Internationale*, based in Paris, which officially monitors all aviation record attempts.
NAS	Naval Air Station.
NASC	Naval Air Systems Command, established 1 May 1966.
NATC	Naval Air Test Center, the flight test facility at Patuxent River, Maryland.
PR	Photo Reconnaissance; also Recce.
Recce	Slang for reconnaissance. Pronounced "recky."
Red Crown	A radar-warning and fighter-direction ship stationed in the Tonkin Gulf on a rotational basis during the Vietnam War.
ResCAP	Rescue Combat Air Patrol.
SAM	Surface-to-Air Missile.
Section	A two-plane flight, sometimes called an element. Two sections compose a four-plane division.
TarCAP	Target Combat Air Patrol. Fighter escort for bombers near the target.
Trap	An arrested landing, usually aboard a carrier, but occasionally on a runway equipped with arresting gear.
VA	An attack aircraft or squadron.
VAH	Heavy attack aircraft or squadron.
VF	Fighter aircraft or squadron.
VFP	Literally fighter-photo, but interpreted as light photo aircraft or squadron because these units fly fighters modified as recon planes.
VMCJ	Marine Composite Utility aircraft or squadron; generally a photo unit.
VMF(AW)	Marine fighter squadron (all weather).

Other U.S.
Aircraft

G

A-1   The Douglas Skyraider, a single-engine propeller-driven attack aircraft also known as the "Spad." Active in the U.S. Navy from 1946 to 1968.

A-3   The Douglas Skywarrior, a twin-jet attack aircraft adaptable to tanker and ECM duties. Affectionately called the "Whale" for its large size. Entered squadron service in 1956.

A-4   The Douglas Skyhawk, a small, single-engine jet attack aircraft sometimes called "Heinemann's Hotrod" after its designer. Entered squadron service in 1956.

A-5   The North American Vigilante, a sophisticated, high-performance jet attack and reconnaissance aircraft operational from 1961 to 1979.

A-6   The Grumman Intruder, a twin-engine, two-seat jet all-weather strike aircraft, also adaptable to ECM and tanker roles. Active since 1963.

A-7   Vought's Corsair II attack plane, a single-engine, single-seat jet with a family resemblance to the Crusader.

Used by the navy and air force since 1966.

AJ The North American Savage, a heavy attack aircraft powered by two piston engines and one jet. Redesignated the A-2, and widely employed as a tanker. Operational from 1949 to 1960.

E-1 A twin-engine, piston-powered early-warning aircraft built by Grumman. The Tracer was operational from 1959 to 1974.

EA-3 The ECM version of the Douglas Sky-warrior.

EA-6 The ECM version of the Grumman Intruder.

EC-121 The Lockheed Constellation, a four-engine prop-driven airliner converted to military use as a flying radar station and ECM base. Operational since 1952.

F-4 The McDonnell Douglas Phantom, originally called F4H by the navy. In navy service since 1960 and air force service since 1962.

F-86 North American's Saber, the premier Korean War fighter developed as a carrier aircraft in the FJ-2 through FJ-4 series by the navy.

F-100 North American's follow-on to the F-86, called the Super Saber.

F-105 The air force's Thunderchief fighter-bomber, a rugged supersonic single-seat, single-engine aircraft built by Republic.

F4D The Douglas Skyray, a single-seat, single-engine jet interceptor operational from 1956 to 1962. Also called the "Ford."

F9F Grumman's single-engine jet fighter series of the 1950s; Panther in the straight-wing, and Cougar in the swept-wing versions. In squadron service from 1949 to 1961.

F11F The Grumman Tiger, a contemporary of the F8U but built in much smaller numbers and operational only from 1957 to 1961.

F2H McDonnell's all-weather twin-engine jet fighter-interceptor, called the Banshee. Active with the navy and marines from 1949 to 1959.

F3H The McDonnell Demon, single-engine, single-seat fighter-interceptor operational from 1956 to 1964.

FJ North American's Fury series. Straight-wing FJ-1s were operational from 1947 to 1949, and swept-wing FJ-2 through -4s were flown by the navy and marines from 1954 to 1962. A relative of the F-86.

KA-3 Tanker version of the Douglas Skywarrior.

KA-6 Grumman's Intruder equipped with underwing fuel tanks for aerial refueling.

RA-5 The recon version of the Vigilante.

Sources and Acknowledgments

This book began at NAS Whidbey Island in September of 1967. As a last fling before starting college, I flew to Oak Harbor, Washington, with my father in our newly restored 1940 navy biplane. At Whidbey's 25th anniversary airshow I met Jerry Unruh, now a rear admiral, a Crusader pilot recently returned from combat. Then a lieutenant, Unruh, one of the great F-8 jocks, gave me his survival knife/shroud-line cutter, and I still fly with it.

That was the first time I gave much thought to the Crusader. But it planted a seed in the back of my mind, a seed that began to sprout ten years later. In August of 1977, again north of Seattle with the N3N, I was one of a group of antiquers attending the Abbotsford, British Columbia, airshow. Following the show, most of the pilots made the rounds of the inevitably loud, cheerful parties. We talked shop, swapped stories, and met new friends.

One of those I met was Tom Weinel, a former F-8 pilot. When I mentioned I might be interested in writing a book about the Crusader, he unzipped a big grin, as if letting me in on a secret. "Don't count on much help," he said. "Near as I remember, nobody bothered to write anything down." Two years later those words bounced off the walls of my memory, where the echo still rings. If Tom hadn't been precisely on target, at least he scored a telling shot. For reasons that remain obscure, the Crusader story has been more difficult to pull together than my four previous books combined. The indifference encountered at many levels was first puzzling, then frustrating. There were times when I despaired of finishing the book.

Yet now and then—just often enough to keep up my morale—some blessed soul took pity on me. One of the earliest was Captain Lonny "Eagle" McClung, skipper of the Navy Fighter Weapons School. He willingly lent what assistance regulations allowed, while dispensing full encouragement. Then my good friend and mentor, retired Vice Admiral Bill Martin, went to bat for me. He contacted one of his former Sixth Fleet helicopter pilots and put me in touch with Lieutenant Commander Gordon Peterson in DOD Public Affairs. Commander Peterson accomplished in one phone call what the combined agencies of the U.S. Government hadn't done in the previous eight months.

Two other official sources were Lieutenant Dale E. Smith, editor of the naval aviation safety magazine *Approach*, and the Naval Air Systems Command with Mr. Al Frascella and Dr. William J. Armstrong. Involved almost from the beginning were Mr. Wes Pryce of the office of naval aviation history, and my friend and colleague, Captain "Zip" Rausa of *Naval Aviation News*. Both lent what information and resources their respective offices allowed. Dr. Dean C. Allard's ever-ready Operational Archives also helped with some documentation.

Among Vought personnel, my initial contact was Art Schoeni, the company's retired photographer. As before, Art's knowledge and enthusiasm carried me over some of the rough spots.

201

The Crusader's designer, Russ Clark, kindly took time to write twice from Dallas where he maintained a busy schedule as a private aerospace consultant. Eldon Corkill dug out old accounts of MiG kills which would otherwise have probably eluded me. Bob Rostine, an early F8U test pilot, offered encouragement with the project but, sadly, he died before the Crusader book really got going, since I was writing my F4U volume at the time. But late in the project, Tommy Wilson of Vought's public affairs office learned of my plight and, in the best Texas tradition, came to the rescue in the nick of time.

Another member of the aerospace industry who lent information and support was Grumman's Washington representative, Ralph Clark. Considering that Vought knocked Grumman out of the fighter business for many years, Ralph's enthusiasm deserves a nod for professionalism. After all, does Macy's tell Gimbels?

Others who lent a hand but were not directly involved with the Crusader included Ensign Rick Morgan. Lou Drendel, well known to aviation buffs for his series of monographs on Vietnam War aircraft, lent numerous photos. Others helping with illustrations were Rowland P. Gill, Nick Williams, and Fred Johnsen of Bomber Books. Captain R. W. Schaffert provided photos, recollections, and documents in abundance. Norman Polmar offered documentary assistance from his voluminous naval aviation files while working on two other books of his own.

Deserving a paragraph to himself is Bob Lawson, the long-suffering yet tireless editor of the Tailhook Association magazine. *The Hook* is what keeps the carrier navy's fraternal organization together, and Bob *is The Hook*.

Foreign assistance came from France and England. As with my previous history of the Corsair, Rear Admiral Pierre Menettrier, the French naval attaché, took an active interest in the Cru-

There's a little Blue Angel in every fighter pilot. Two F-8Js of VF-191 indulge in some impromptu revelry, enjoying the sheer thrill of flying. "Satan's Kittens" made eight Tonkin Gulf deployments, four in Oriskany (CVA 34). (U.S. Navy)

sader project. And British aviation writer Bill Gunston kindly recounted his 1962 discussion with a Soviet aviation official.

Those navy, marine, and Vought contributors who had direct involvement with the Crusader are listed below. But several deserve additional recognition. The first was Bob Dosé, who provided exceptional assistance and cheerfully recounted his days as skipper of VX-3. Much of the manuscript was written during the rain and snow of a dreary Oregon winter, and the memory of Bob and Betty Dosé's warm hos-

203

The Crusader III in flight with ventral fins lowered to provide additional stability at higher speeds. (Vought)

pitality (not to mention their heated backyard whirlpool) took some of the edge off the chill.

The marines were ably represented by retired Colonel Roger Peard, who penned numerous letters about his BuAer job with the F-8 between dealing hands of Twenty-One at Lake Tahoe. Commander Cole Pierce matched Peard's page count with a thick package of reflections on VF-211, and the best description I've seen of the problems in landing an F-8. MiG killers Bobby Lee, John Nichols, and Jerry Tucker described their successful combats in detail. The reserves came through in fine style, thanks to Commander Peter Mersky and Lieutenant Tom Nelson of VFP-306.

Additionally, I'm indebted to retired Rear Admiral Bill Leonard, my best and most valued critic, for reading portions of the manuscript. Vice Admiral Jim Stockdale read the book as well. And so did retired Captain Joe Rees, who livened the "Naval Aviators' Annual Elk Hunt"

with his reflections on the early F8U program at BuAer. Marion Carl, who never misses, and John Wheatley, ace muleskinner, also recalled their tours at Pax River. Among the other stalwarts at Table Springs were Bill Meyring, who kept the biscuits coming, and Butch Davenport, resident philosopher and fire-starter.

Finally, a dip of the wing in salute to VFP-63, "The Eyes of the Fleet." Commander Dennis "Taco" Bell and his troops were much in evidence at the 1979 meeting of the Tailhook Association, and there was no doubt where "Crusader Corner" was established. Some of the pilots toted in a large-scale RF-8 model with all the fervor of a band of religious zealots parading a sacred icon. Such were their feelings for the Crusader. An invitation to visit "Fightin' Photo" was gratefully accepted, and the subsequent trip to Miramar proved as informative as it was enjoyable. Taco Bell and company couldn't do enough to sell me on their bird. And though

A NASA Crusader modified with a super-critical wing for experimental research. (Williams)

205

VFP-63 was in no way involved, they even apologized for the loss of the only two-seat Crusader, saying I really should have had a flight in it.

No argument, gentlemen. No argument.

Following is a list of those contributors who have had official association with the Crusader. Ranks are either those held at retirement, or current grade. Assignments reflect the individual's affiliation with the F-8, whether past or present.

Sources

Captain Dennis J. Bell, USN(Ret.)	CO, VFP-63
Mr. Allen W. Cater	VF-103
Mr. John Russell Clark	Vought
Mr. Eldon Corkill	Vought
Captain Robert G. Dosé, USN(Ret.)	CO, VX-3
Commander Norman A. Gandia, USN(Ret.)	VF-33
Rear Admiral Bobby C. Lee, USN	VF-24
Rear Admiral William N. Leonard, USN(Ret.)	NATC and CO, USS *Ranger*
Captain Lonny McClung, USN(Ret.)	CO, Navy Fighter Weapons School
Rear Admiral Pierre Menettrier (Ret.)	French Navy
Commander Peter Mersky, USNR	ACIO, VFP-306
Lieutenant Thomas P. Nelson, USNR	PAO, VFP-306
Commander John B. Nichols III, USN(Ret.)	VF-194
Captain Jack Patton, USMC (Ret.)	VMF-235
Colonel Roger Peard, USMC (Ret.)	Bureau of Aeronautics
Commander Joseph T. Phaneuf	XO, VFP-63
Commander Cole Pierce, USN	VF-211
Rear Admiral James D. Ramage, USN(Ret.)	CO, USS *Independence*
Captain Joe Rees, USN(Ret.)	Bureau of Aeronautics
Captain R. W. Schaffert, USN(Ret.)	VF-111
Vice Admiral James B. Stockdale, USN(Ret.)	Commander Air Wing 16
Commander Gerald D. Tucker, USN(Ret.)	VF-211
Mr. Tom Weinel	VF-162
Mr. Roger Wenschlag	VF-211, VF-124
Captain R. W. Windsor, USN(Ret.)	Naval Air Test Center

Notes

Chapter One

1. Correspondence with Bill Gunston, 11 March 1980.
2. Interview with John Wheatley, November 1979.
3. Correspondence with Boone Guyton, November 1978.
4. Correspondence with W. N. Leonard, April 1980.
5. Correspondence with J. R. Clark, 5 October 1979.
6. Ibid.
7. Ibid.
8. Leonard, op. cit.
9. Clark, op. cit.
10. Clark, correspondence of 15 April 1980.
11. Tom Wolfe, *The Right Stuff*, p. 253.

Chapter Two

1. Telephone interview with Ralph Clark, 31 March 1980.
2. Correspondence with Cole Pierce, 8 January 1980.
3. Ibid.
4. Ibid.
5. Interview with Robert G. Dosé, February 1979.
6. Ibid.
7. Ibid.
8. *Naval Aviation News*, April 1957.
9. Telephone interview with Woody Cater, 29 June 1979.
10. MCAS Yuma news release, August 1975.
11. John F. Kennedy to VFP-62, 26 January 1963.

12. Correspondence with Roger Wenschlag, 3 August 1979.
13. Papers of Art Schoeni.
14. *Naval Aviation News*, January 1976.
15. Ibid.

Chapter Three

1. "Crusader," *Air Classics*, November 1978.
2. Details on tracking Project One Grand from *Chance Vought News*, September 1956.
3. Dosé interview, February 1979.
4. *Vought Vanguard*, 17 July 1957.
5. *Crusader Fighter Report*, October 1974.

Chapter Four

1. Interview with Tom Weinel, March 1980.
2. Correspondence with Roger Peard, 20 January 1980.
3. Correspondence with Bobby C. Lee, 28 March 1980.
4. VAdm. Malcolm W. Cagle, "TF-77 in Action off Vietnam," U.S. Naval Institute *Proceedings*, May 1972. p. 104.
5. Pierce correspondence.
6. Weinel interview.

Chapter Five

1. Norman Polmar, *Aircraft Carriers*, p. 674.
2. Cagle, "TF-77 in Action", p. 73.
3. Pierce correspondence.
4. Cagle, "TF-77 in Action", p. 73–74.
5. Correspondence with Jack Patton, 11 October 1979.
6. Dewey Weddell and Norman Wood, *Air War Vietnam*, p. 42.
7. Ibid., p. 46.
8. Ibid., p. 50.
9. Frank Harvey, "Air War in Vietnam," *Flying*, November 1966.
10. Weinel interview, March 1980.
11. VF-191 history.
12. Pierce correspondence.

Chapter Six

1. Interview with Robin Olds, May 1975.
2. Correspondence with Bobby Lee, 28 March 1980.

3. R. Braybrook, *Flying Review International.* November 1965.
4. *Grumman Horizons*, vol. 8, no. 1, p. 11.
5. Ibid.
6. Ibid.
7. Ibid.
8. Ibid., p. 6.
9. Associated Press report, 14 June 1966.
10. *Grumman Horizons*, p. 8.
11. *Popular Aviation*, September–October 1967, p. 46.
12. Ibid.
13. Ibid.
14. Ibid.
15. Lee correspondence, 12 March 1980.
16. Pierce correspondence.
17. Ibid.
18. Lee correspondence.
19. Ibid.
20. *Naval Aviation News*, December 1977.
21. Ibid.
22. Correspondence with R. W. Schaffert, 20 July 1979.
23. Ibid.
24. Ibid.
25. Ibid.
26. Ibid.
27. *Bon Homme Richard* news release, No. 63–68.
28. Ibid.
29. Ibid.
30. Correspondence with John B. Nichols, 14 December 1979.
31. Ibid.
32. Ibid.
33. Ibid.
34. Ibid.
35. *Bon Homme Richard* newspaper, August 1968.
36. Ibid.
37. Ibid.
38. Weinel interview, March 1980.
39. Ibid.
40. Correspondence with Jerry Tucker, 30 April 1980.
41. Ibid.

Chapter Seven

1. The two-seater is usually listed as the 74th aircraft, owing to the first three F8U-1Ps.

2. *Flying Review International*, July 1964.
3. Correspondence with Pierre Menettrier, 3 May 1980.
4. Profile Publication Number 90.
5. Naval Aviation Safety Center statistics, cited at the Sixth Last Annual Crusader Ball, 21 May 1988.
6. Correspondence with Norman Gandia, 16 May 1980.
7. Ibid.
8. Nichols correspondence, 14 December 1979.

Bibliography

Books

Drendel, Lou . . . *And Kill MiGs*. Warren, MI: Squadron-Signal Publications, 1974.
  F-8 Crusader in Action. Warren, MI: Squadron-Signal Publications, 1973.

Joos, Gerhard. Profile Number 90. *The Chance-Vought F-8A to F-8E Crusader*. Leatherhead, Surrey, England: Profile Publications, 1966.

Polmar, Norman, *Aircraft Carriers*. New York: Doubleday, 1969.

Sambito, W. J. *A History of Marine Attack Squadron 312*. Washington, D.C.: U.S. Marine Corps, 1978.

Weddell, Dewey, and Norman Wood, eds. *Air War Vietnam*. New York: Arno Books, 1978.

Wolfe, Tom. *The Right Stuff*. New York: Farrar, Strauss & Giroux, 1979.

U.S. Navy. *U.S. Naval Aviation 1910–1970*. Washington, D.C.: Government Printing Office, 1970.

Periodicals

Cagle, VAdm. Malcolm C. "TF-77 in Action off Vietnam." U.S. Naval Institute *Proceedings* (May 1972).

Chance Vought News "F8U Sets New U.S. Speed Mark" (September 1956).

Crusader Fighter Report. October 1974. Summary of F-8 operations.

Cunningham, PH2 Doug. "The Crusaders." *Naval Aviation News* (September 1976).

Flying Review International. "The MiG-21 Fishbed" (November 1963). "Bloodlines of a Champion Crusader" (July 1964). "The Perennial MiG-17" (September 1964). "Weapons and Systems" (June 1965).

Harvey, Frank. "Air War in Vietnam." *Flying* (November 1966).

Kelley, Lt. Daniel W., Jr. "Moments and MiGs." *Naval Aviation News* (December 1977).

McCutcheon, Lt. Gen. Keith. "Marine Aviation in Vietnam." U.S. Naval Institute *Proceedings* (May 1971).

Marr, Cdr. H. L. "We Will Get MiGs." *Grumman Horizons.* Vol 8., no. 1.

Miller, Jay. "Crusader Without a Cause." *Airpower* (July 1977).

Naval Aviation News. "*Bullet* Sets Records" (April 1957). "FIP Report" (October 1957).

Schoeni, Arthur L. "Crusader." *Air Classics* (November 1977).

Scholin, Allin. "Crusaders Get New Lease on Life." *Air Progress* (April 1969).

Vampatella, Lt. L. P. "Tally Ho! MiGs!" *Popular Aviation* (September/October 1967).

Vought Aeronautics. "The Crusader Story" (circa 1960).

Vought Vanguard. "F8U Smashes Coast-to-Coast Record" (17 July 1957).

Index

The Naval Institute Press is the book-publishing arm of the U.S. Naval Institute, a private, non-profit professional society for members of the sea services and civilians who share an interest in naval and maritime affairs. Established in 1873 at the U.S. Naval Academy in Annapolis, Maryland, where its offices remain today, the Naval Institute has more than 100,000 members worldwide.

Members of the Naval Institute receive the influential monthly naval magazine *Proceedings* and substantial discounts on fine nautical prints, ship and aircraft photos, and subscriptions to the Institute's recently inaugurated quarterly, *Naval History*. They also have access to the transcripts of the Institute's Oral History Program and may attend any of the Institute-sponsored seminars regularly offered around the country.

The book-publishing program, begun in 1898 with basic guides to naval practices, has broadened its scope in recent years to include books of more general interest. Now the Naval Institute Press publishes more than forty new titles each year, ranging from how-to books on boating and navigation to battle histories, biographies, ship guides, and novels. Institute members receive discounts on the Press's more than 300 books.

For a free catalog describing books currently available and for further information about U.S. Naval Institute membership, please write to:

Membership Department
U.S. Naval Institute
Annapolis, Maryland 21402

or call, toll-free, 800-233-USNI.

THE NAVAL INSTITUTE PRESS

MiG MASTER

The Story of the F-8 Crusader

This book was set in 10/13 Baskerville with
Optima display type by NK Graphics,
Baltimore, Maryland.
It is printed on 60-lb. Glatfelter
Glatco matte and bound in Holliston Roxite B cloth
by The Maple Press Company, York,
Pennsylvania.